T0101444

NELSON'S
MINISTER'S
MANUAL
NKJV EDITION

THOMAS NELSON
Since 1798

NASHVILLE   DALLAS   MEXICO CITY   RIO DE JANEIRO

© 2003 by Thomas Nelson, Inc.

All rights reserved. No portion of this book may be reproduced, stored in a retrieval system, or transmitted in any form by any means—electronic, mechanical, photocopy, recording, scanning, or other—except for brief quotations in critical reviews or articles, without the prior written permission of the publisher.

Published in Nashville, TN, by Thomas Nelson. Thomas Nelson is a trademark of Thomas Nelson, Inc.

Thomas Nelson, Inc. titles may be purchased in bulk for educational, business, fund-raising, or sales promotional use. For information, please email SpecialMarkets@Thomas Nelson.com.

Unless otherwise indicated, Scripture quotations are from the New King James Version of the Bible, © 1982 by Thomas Nelson, Inc., Publishers.

Book design and composition by ProtoType Graphics, Nashville, Tennessee.

Nelson's minister's manual, NKJV edition
  Joshua Rowe (ed.)
  ISBN 10: 0-7852-5089-1
  ISBN 13: 978-0-7852-5089-0

Printed in the United States of America

23 24 25 26 27 LBC 26 25 24 23 22

Table of Contents

Contributors

Jerry Carraway
Minister of music, The Donelson Fellowship, Nashville, Tennessee

> Favorite Wedding Hymns
> Traditional Funeral Hymns
> Worship Design Worksheet

Rev. Mark Hollis
Freelance writer; former minister of 15 years

> Issues to Address in Premarital Counseling
> Sample Graveside/Committal Services
> Vow Renewal Ceremony

Dr. William H. Jones
Faculty member, Columbia International University, Columbia, South Carolina; president of Crossover Communications International

> Alternative Witnessing Plan

Rev. Todd Kinde
Pastor of Grace Bible Church, Grandville, Michigan

> Agape Meal/Communion Service
> Baptism Sermon
> Baptism Service for Professing Adults and Children
> Sample Wedding Ceremony: Formal
> Wedding Sermon: For a Second Marriage

Rev. Robert J. Morgan
Writer; pastor of The Donelson Fellowship, Nashville, Tennessee

> Funeral Sermon: Accident Victim
> Invitations (all sections)
> Wedding Sermon: General
> Wedding Sermon: Informal/Home

Rev. Richard Sharpe
President and director of Small Church Ministries, Christian Home Crusade

> Child/Infant Dedication
> Communion Sermon
> Funeral Sermon: Child or Youth
> Funeral Sermon: Non-Christian
> Funeral Sermon: Suicide Victim

Dr. Charles A. Thigpen
Promotional director, Tennessee State Association of Free Will Baptists

> Home Visitation Checklist
> Hospital Visitation Checklist
> Traditional Verses to Share with the Sick or Dying

Dr. Melvin Worthington
Executive secretary, National Association of Free Will Baptists

> Building Dedication
> Groundbreaking Service
> Home Dedication
> Installation/Consecration Service
> Ordination of Deacons
> Ordination of Ministers
> Sample Funeral Service
> Sample Wedding Ceremony: Informal

All additional material is the result of the research and ministry of the general editor, Joshua D. Rowe. Special thanks to my wife, Grace, for all your patience and support.

Editor's Preface

The crowd has gathered, and family members and friends have seated themselves in neat rows, whispering quietly. Young men and women take their places down front, dressed in once-in-a-lifetime attire. Organ fanfare heralds the arrival of a figure dressed all in white. A hush falls over the room, and everyone awaits the first words of the minister:

"Dearly beloved, we are gathered here in the sight of God . . ."

The words are familiar—and somehow reassuring—but how does the minister know what he is supposed to say in such a situation?

Weddings may not be a daily occurrence, but they are definitely part of the professional routine of every minister. Likewise funerals occur with all too great a frequency. Hospital visitation with the sick and dying—infant dedications—deacon ordinations—communion services—these and many other events are regular parts of a minister's routine. *Nelson's Minister's Manual* has been designed to offer fresh, timely material to help in planning services and delivering appropriate sermons.

Of course not every wedding is the same. Some are elaborate affairs, with flowers and candles and "all the trimmings." Others may be quite simple, performed before a cluster of family members in a home. And the minister's charge may be worded differently if he is facing a mid-life couple renewing their vows instead of a pair of fresh-faced kids starting a new life together. You will find help for each of these situations in this manual.

Funerals also call for different approaches, depending upon the circumstances. In this manual you will find five sample sermons, each appropriate in speaking to different needs. Likewise the graveside service suggestions here differ according to whether the person being buried was a believer or not, and depending on whether the graveside service is in addition to or in place of the traditional funeral.

A wealth of traditional Scripture verses have been collected for you in the Weddings, Funerals, and Pastoral Care sections. Hymns are suggested throughout, with a list of favorites included under Weddings and Funerals.

You will find much, much more in this little book—so much that we believe you will want to get at least two copies—one to keep at your desk and one for the glove compartment of your car. Take a few moments right now to discover the wealth of practical helps this manual offers right at your fingertips.

Weddings

Issues to Address in Premarital Counseling
By Rev. Mark Hollis, M. A.

The following is a guide and an outline of six premarital counseling sessions. It is not, however, an exhaustive tool by which any minister may become a counselor. Before the minister attempts to counsel any couple, he should have spent a good deal of time in study, in observing professional Christian counseling, and in prayer and meditation on the subject; it is not a responsibility to be taken lightly.

Use these six topics to guide you in collecting resources for the ministry of pre-marriage counseling. You may wish to take advantage of a personality inventory for use with couples preparing for marriage.

Topics for Premarital Counseling:
- Introduction and Faith
- Personality Issues, Expectations, and Roles
- Family Issues
- Communication and Conflict Resolution
- Finances
- Sex

When first contacted, ask the couple to complete this form. Provide a self-addressed stamped envelope for the couple to return it to you.

So You Want To Get Married!—Some things you need to know:

You will be expected to complete at least six sessions of premarital preparation.

You will be expected to attend worship at our church from the time we initiate counseling through the first month of your marriage. Exceptions are made only for couples living out of town that are attending a church there during preparation for the wedding.

You will be expected to complete all homework for each session.

Please complete the following information:

Bride: Age:

Groom: Age:

Is the woman pregnant?

Have you been married before?

Bride:

Groom:

Do you have children from this or a previous relationship?

Bride:

Groom:

Why would you like to get married at this time?

Bride:

Groom:

Complete and return this form in the envelope provided one week prior to our first meeting.

Session One: Introduction and Faith—Aim: To get to know the couple and encourage them to center their marriage on Jesus Christ.

Procedure:

1. Ask the couple to share with you the story of their courtship:

> How did you meet?
> Why are you coming to get married at this time?

2. What has been the reaction of your family and friends to your plans to marry?

3. Explain to the couple the plan of salvation urging them to come to personal relationship with Christ. If both are believers, encourage them to grow in their faith and center their marriage on Christ.

4. Address any issues that arise in the form above. Let the couple know if you will not be able to perform their marriage. If you have reservations, now is the time to speak up.

Homework: *Opposites List* (Compile a list of ways you and your partner are different. "He is a night owl, while she is a morning person," etc.)

Session Two: Personality Issues, Expectations, and Roles—Aim: To lead the couple to a greater understanding of how differing personalities can add strength as well as create difficulty and to facilitate further discussion of expectations and roles.

Procedure:

1. Ask partners to separately list ten reasons why they love their partner. Have them share their list verbally by turning toward their partner and saying, "I love you because ..."

2. Review the *Opposites List*. Ask them to identify five areas where their differences might cause conflict as well as five areas where differences might be a source of strength.

3. Ask partners to separately list expectations they have of their partner in marriage. ("I expect her to initiate sex;" "I expect him to take responsibility for paying the bills.") Have them exchange sheets and mark with a + those that will be easy to live up to, a – those that will be difficult, and a ? for those they are not sure about.

4. "Which of the following descriptions most closely describes the relationship in the home you grew up in? Which do you hope will describe your own home?" Explain that regardless of our best plans we often revert to conduct that is like that of the home we grew up in:

    Dominant husband with submissive wife: He led. She followed.

    Dominant wife with acquiescing husband: She just let him think he was in charge.

    Leadership by husband with willing wife: She had input, but he had the final say.

    Equal roles: Decisions were made together or not at all.

Session Three: Family of Origin and Family Issues—

Aim: To lead the couple to a greater understanding of how family of origin is likely to effect the way they relate to each other and to get them off to a good start in handling extended family relationships.

Procedure:

1. Read Genesis 2:24. Ask each one to explain their understanding of what it means to "leave" and to "cleave."

2. Ask her to describe his relationship with his parents. Ask him to describe her relationship with her parents. Ask him, "How might her relationship with her father affect your relationship?" Ask her, "How might his relationship with his mother affect your relationship?"

    Ask each partner to indicate which of the following statements best describes their family of origin:

    "In our house mom or dad had dinner ready most days and we usually ate together as a family."

    "In our house mom served dinner at the same time everyday and everyone was expected to be there."

    "In our house we sometimes ate together and sometimes didn't."

    "In our house everyone fended for him or herself when it came to dinnertime."

3. "How might the family you grew up in affect your own manner of relating to one another?"

Homework: *Start Off Right* ("Before the next session, write a letter thanking your future in-laws for helping to make your fiancé or fiancée the person he or she is today. Tell them why you look forward to having them as in-laws. Mail it before the next session.")

Session Four: Communication and Conflict Resolution—Aim: To lead the couple to establish guidelines for good communication as well as a strategy for handling conflict.

Procedure:

1. Keep a model you have built with children's building blocks hidden while you have the couple take seats back to back. Give the man the item you built and the woman the appropriate pieces to replicate the model. The woman is not allowed to see the model or to speak while the man gives her instructions on replicating it. Allow five minutes for building. Reposition the chairs and discuss the futility of one-way communication.

2. Ask the couple to read James 4:1–3. What is the root cause of most marital conflict? (selfish desires) What instruction does James 1:19 give for resolving and avoiding conflict?

3. Share the following five principles for resolving conflict in marriage:

    1. Listen: Instead of demanding that you be heard, listen carefully to the other person (see Proverbs 18:13 and James 1:19).
    2. Select: Select an appropriate time (Ephesians 4:26).
    3. Define: How do you define the problem? How does your partner define the problem?
    4. Discuss: Define the areas of agreement and disagreement in the conflict.

5. Identify: Identify your own contribution to the problem. Acknowledging your own contribution will lead to prompter resolution.

Homework: *You Can Have It All* ("Imagine you have charged $1,000 for your new household on a credit card at an annual interest rate of 18%. How long will it take you to pay it off if you make the minimum payment of about $20.00 each month?" The formula is monthly balance + 1.5% each month – $20.00 and then repeat for each subsequent month.)

Household Budget (Prepare a household budget for review in the next session.)

Session Five: Finances—Aim: To lead the couple to understand scriptural principles for financial management as well as to develop and implement a household budget.

Procedure:

1. Review basic principles for financial management:
   Psalm 24:1—It all belongs to God.
   Luke 21:1–4—Generosity toward God is expected.
   Romans 13:8—Pay your debts, especially the debt of love.

2. Ask partners to separately list, in order of priority, the top ten financial priorities for their household (food, insurance, house payment, church gifts, car payment, etc.) Review and compare differences in list.

3. Review the proposed household budget.

Session Six: The Sexual Relationship—The couple should take advantage of one of the excellent manuals to guide Christian couples in developing a healthy sexual relationship.

Aim: To lead the couple to understand the scriptural foundation of the sexual relationship as well as to initiate healthy and open conversation about the sexual relationship.

Procedure:

1. Ask couple to answer these questions:

    > Where did you get your ideas regarding sex?
    > What was the attitude toward sex in your home?
    > How might the attitude toward sex in your home affect your sexual relationship in marriage?

2. Read 1 Corinthians 7:1–11.

    > Why is marriage a good thing? (vv. 1–2)
    > What responsibility does each partner have toward the other? (vv. 3–4)
    > Why should such abstinence be only for an agreed upon period? (vv. 4–5)

3. Suggestions for a healthy sexual adjustment:

    > Men are visually stimulated while women need tenderness.
    > The drive of one may surpass that of the other, so giving to one another is appropriate.
    > Talk about what you like and don't like.
    > Guard the relationship and keep it private.

Sexually explicit books, magazines, and movies will not help, but harm your sexual relationship.

4. Offer any additional advice, or address any additional issues and close in prayer.

Wedding Registration Form

Date of Wedding: _____

Location of Wedding: _____

_____

Bride: _____

    Religious Affiliation: _____

    Bride's Parents: _____

Groom: _____

    Religious Affiliation: _____

    Groom's Parents: _____

Ceremony to be Planned by Minister: ____ by Couple: ____

Other Minister(s) Assisting: _____

Maid/Matron of Honor: _____

Best Man: _____

Wedding Planner: _____

Date of Rehearsal: _____

Reception Open to All Wedding Guests: _____

By Invitation Only: _____

Location of Reception: _____

Wedding Photos to be Taken: _____ During Ceremony

                               _____ After Ceremony

Date(s) of Counseling: _____

Date of Registration: _____

Sample Wedding Ceremony: Formal
By Rev. Todd Kinde

A Sample Formal Wedding Ceremony Order of Service

Seating

Prelude Music

Processional

Call to Worship

Invocation

Charge

Giving of the Bride

Declaration of Intent

Ascend the Platform

Scripture Reading

Solo Music

Homily

Vows

Ring Ceremony

Lighting of the Unity Candle

Declaration

Pronouncement

Prayer

Kiss

Presentation

Recessional

Dismissal

Signing of the License

Clean-up

Reception

Photos

A Sample Detailed Formal
Wedding Ceremony

Seating: *Spend some time with the ushers at rehearsal to give them instruction. Traditionally the bride's family is seated on the left side of the sanctuary and the groom's family is seated on the right side of the sanctuary. As the ushers escort the women to their seat they should walk on the right side of women, with the usher's left arm bent to hold the woman's right arm. The ushers should walk at a slower pace than usual to accommodate high-healed shoes and flowing dresses.*

Prelude Music: *Appropriate wedding music should be played as the congregation assembles.*

Processional: *Pastor takes position at the center of lower platform area.*

The ushers seat the mothers first; music which may be used during the seating of the mothers includes Jesu, Joy of Man's Desiring.

Next is the seating of the bridal party. The groom's men and bride's maids may enter together or the groom's men may take position at the platform entering from a side room while the bride's maids enter from the center aisle.

Finally, the bride comes down the aisle; the traditional music used is the Bridal Chorus, *but may be an appropriate song chosen by the bride and groom. Her father or another family representative may escort her. The people should stand as the bride enters.*

Call to Worship: We are gathered here to worship God and to witness the marriage vows of

Groom's Full Name and *Bride's Full Name.*

Let your light so shine before people that they may see your good works and give glory to your Father who is in heaven.

Invocation: Living, Triune God, for grace we come. May this ceremony be pleasing in Your sight and bring to us Your blessing. Amen.

Charge: Dearly beloved, we are gathered together in the sight of God to join together this man and woman in holy matrimony. It is an honorable estate, instituted of God, signifying unto us the mystical union that is between Christ and His church, that holy estate Christ adorned and beautified with His presence and first miracle in Cana of Galilee. It is commended in the Scriptures to be honorable among all, and therefore is not by any to be entered into unadvisedly or lightly, but reverently, discreetly, advisedly, soberly, and in the fear of God. Into this holy estate these two persons present come now to be joined.

Giving of the Bride

Pastor: Who will give this woman to be married to this man?

Father: Her Mother and I.

If the parents are not giving the bride, another phrase may be used such as,

Her mother and our family.
Her family.

The congregation is then seated.

Declaration of Intent: *Groom's Full Name* will you take *Bride's Full Name* to be your wedded wife, to live together after God's ordinance in the holy estate of matrimony? Will you love her, comfort her, honor and keep her, in sickness and in health, and forsaking all others, keep yourself only unto her, so long as you both shall live? Please respond, "I will."

The groom says, I will.

Bride's Full Name will you take *Groom's Full Name* to be your wedded husband, to live together after God's ordinance in the holy estate of matrimony? Will you love him, comfort him, honor and keep him, in sickness and in health, and forsaking all others, keep yourself only unto him, so long as you both shall live? Please respond, "I will."

The bride says, I will.

The wedding party will now ascend the platform.

Scripture Reading: *The Scripture reading may be one that is meaningful to the couple being married or one that has been used as a basis for premarital counseling.*

Therefore, as the elect of God, holy and beloved, put on tender mercies, kindness, humility, meekness, longsuffering; bearing with one another, and forgiving one another, if anyone has a complaint against another; even as Christ forgave you, so you also must do. But above all these things put on love, which is the bond of perfection. And let the peace of God rule in your hearts, to which also you were called in one body; and be thankful. Let the word of Christ dwell in you richly in all wisdom, teaching and admonishing one another in psalms and hymns and spiritual songs, singing with grace in your hearts to the Lord (Colossians 3:12–16).

Solo Music: *The solo should be relevant and meaningful to the bride and groom; since the wedding party remains standing, the song should not be longer than two or three minutes.*

Homily

Vows: *Minister places bride's hand in groom's right hand and asks the groom to repeat after him:*

I, *Groom's First Name,* take thee, *Bride's First Name,*
to be my wedded wife,
to have and to hold from this day forward,
for better for worse, for richer for poorer,
in sickness and in health, to love and to cherish,
till death us do part,
according to God's holy ordinance;
and there to do I give thee my pledge.

Groom releases bride's hand, and bride takes groom's right hand and repeats after minister:

I, *Bride's First Name,* take thee, *Groom's First Name,*
to be my wedded husband,
to have and to hold from this day forward,

for better for worse, for richer for poorer,
in sickness and in health, to love and to cherish,
till death us do part,
according to God's holy ordinance;
and there to do I give thee my pledge.

Ring Ceremony: As a token of this covenant, you will now give and receive the marriage rings. The unbroken circle, the emblem of eternity, and the gold, the emblem of that which is least tarnished and most enduring, are to show how lasting is the pledge you have each made to the other.

The bride will give her flowers to the maid of honor. The maid of honor will give the ring to the bride while the best man will give the ring to the groom. The bride and groom will place the rings on the minister's Bible. The minister will pray,

Bless, O Lord, these rings that as *Groom's First Name* and *Bride's First Name* wear them they may abide in Your peace and continue in Your favor, unto their life's end, through Jesus Christ our Lord. Amen.

Give the bride's ring to groom. The groom will take the bride's left hand and place the ring on her third finger. Holding it there, he will repeat after the minister,

With this ring I thee wed, in the name of the Father and of the Son and of the Holy Spirit. Amen.

Give the groom's ring to bride. The bride will take the groom's left hand and place the ring on his third finger. Holding it there she will repeat after the minister,

With this ring I thee wed, in the name of the Father and of the Son and of the Holy Spirit. Amen.

Lighting of the Unity Candle: The bride and groom move to the unity candle and light it together. The maid of honor should ensure the train of the bride's dress is smoothly flowing behind the bride. The couple may kneel to pray. A musical piece or solo may occur at this time of reflection and prayer. When the prayer is completed the couple will move back to position in front of the minister. Again the maid of honor should ensure the bride's dress is in order.

Declaration: Minister will now join the couple's right hands together and say,

Those whom God has joined together let no one put asunder.

Pronouncement: For as much as *Groom's First Name* and *Bride's First Name* have consented together in holy wedlock, and have witnessed the same before God and this congregation, and in so doing have given and pledged their vows to each other, and have declared the same by the giving and receiving of a ring, I pronounce them man and wife together, in the Name of Father, and of the Son, and of the Holy Spirit. Amen.

Prayer: O God, who has so consecrated the state of marriage that in it is represented the spiritual marriage and unity between Christ and His church: Look mercifully upon these Your cherished servants. May they love, honor and cherish each other, and so live together in faithfulness and patience, in wisdom and true godliness, that their home may be a haven of blessing and of peace. We pray this through Jesus Christ, our Lord, who lives and reigns with Thee and the Holy Spirit, One God, world without end. Amen.

Kiss: You may now kiss the bride!

Presentation: I present to you Mr. and Mrs. *Groom's First Name and Last Name!*

Recessional: *The bride and groom will exit down the center aisle with a quicker pace and a sense of joy. Traditionally,* The Wedding March *should be played. The wedding party may follow.*

Dismissal and Receiving Line: *The ushers may dismiss the people beginning with the brides family in the front and then the groom's family in the front. The remaining quests may be dismissed row-by-row, alternating from side to side. The ushers should observe the line greeting the newly married couple and wait to dismiss another row when the line is long.*

Some couples prefer to re-enter the sanctuary and dismiss the guests themselves while greeting them at the same time.

In either procedure the greeting time is often longer than the ceremony itself.

Signing of the License: *The two witness should be assembled, one for the bride and one for the groom, to sign* *the marriage license. Some couples like to have a photograph of the signing and like to use a special pen as a keepsake. The minister is responsible to sign the license as well and to ensure that it is delivered to the proper civil authorities for recording. Be sure to read the specific instructions for your city, county, or state.*

Clean-up

Reception: *The minister is traditionally invited to the reception, and should attend if at all possible.*

Photos: *Wedding photos may be done before or after the ceremony. Sometimes photos are taken both times and even during the ceremony itself.*

A Sample Wedding Ceremony: Informal
By Dr. Melvin Worthington

A Sample Informal Wedding Ceremony Order of Service

Prelude	*Declaration of Vows*
Solos	*Exchange of Rings*
Entrance of Mothers	*Prayer*
Entrance of Bridal Party	*Ceremony of Candles*
The Ceremony	*Presentation of Bride and Groom*
Prayer	*Recessional*
Solo	

A Sample Detailed Informal Wedding Ceremony

Prelude: *Appropriate wedding music should be played as the congregation assembles. If the wedding is held in a pastor's office or a home, music may not be necessary, or may be played from a tape or cd.*

Solos: *Special music may be rendered at this point. Some songs which can be used are* Together, Always, And I Love You So.

Entrance of Mothers: *The ushers seat the mothers at this point. Music which may be used during the seating of the mothers includes* Jesu, Joy of Man's Desiring.

Entrance of Bridal Party: *Music which may be used during the entrance of the bridal party includes* Trumpet Voluntary (Prince of Denmark's March) *and* Bridal Chorus.

The Ceremony: *When the persons to be married have presented themselves to the minister the ceremony can begin. The minister shall say:*

Friends and family members, we have the pleasure of seeing these two persons present themselves before God and these witnesses for the purpose of being united in the holy bonds of matrimony. Therefore, if any person can show just cause why these two may not lawfully be joined together as husband and wife, let him now speak, or forever hereafter hold his peace.

Marriage is a divine, distinctive, designed, directed and enduring institution, instituted by Almighty God, and given to man in a state of innocence and happiness. Hear the divine record of the first marriage in human history, *And the* Lord *God said, "It is not good that man should be alone; I will make him a helper comparable to him." Out of the ground the* Lord *God formed every beast of the field and every bird of the air, and brought them to Adam to see what he would call them. And whatever Adam called each living creature, that was its name. So Adam gave names to all cattle, to the birds of the air, and to every beast of the field. But for Adam there was not found a helper comparable to him. And the* Lord *God caused a deep sleep to fall on Adam, and he slept; and He took one of his ribs, and closed up the flesh in its place. Then the rib which the* Lord *God had taken from man He made into a woman, and He brought her to the man. And Adam said: "This is now bone of my bones and flesh of my flesh; she shall be called Woman, because she was taken out of man." Therefore a man shall leave his father and mother and be joined to his wife, and they shall become one flesh. And they were both naked, the man and his wife, and were not ashamed* (Genesis 2:18–25).

God gives specific directions and regulations for the government of the marriage estate. Paul addresses this when he says, *Wives submit to you own husbands, as to the Lord. For the husband is head of the wife, as also Christ is head of the church; and He is the Savior of the body. Therefore, just as the church is subject to Christ, so let the wives be to their own husbands in everything. Husbands, love your wives, just as Christ also loved the church and gave Himself for her, that He might sanctify and cleanse her with the washing of water by the word, that He might present her to Himself a glorious church, not having spot or wrinkle or any such thing, but that she should be holy and without blemish. So husbands ought to love their own wives as their own bodies; he who loves his wife loves himself. For no one ever hated his own flesh, but nourishes and cherishes it, just as the Lord does the church. For we are members of His body, of His flesh and of His bones. "For this reason a man shall leave his father and mother and be joined to his wife, and the two shall become one flesh." This is a great mystery, but I speak concerning Christ and the church. Nevertheless let each one of you in particular so love his own wife as himself, and let the wife see that she respects her husband* (Ephesians 5:22–33).

Prayer: Lord, we ask you to be glorified in this service, in Jesus' name and for His sake, Amen.

Solo: *Following the minister's prayer a soloist may sing an appropriate song.*

Declaration of Vows

Minister: If, with confident trust in each other, you are now ready to accept each other as husband and wife to pursue life's journey together, you will acknowledge this decision of hearts by taking each other by the *right hand*.

"Do you, M_____, take N_____, whom you hold by the hand, to be your true and lawful wife, to love and cherish her, in joy or pain, in sickness or health and forsaking all others, to cleave to her only, so long as you both live?"

Answer: I do.

Minister: "Do you, N_____, take M_____, whom you hold by the hand, to be your lawful and true husband, to love, honor, obey and cherish him, in joy or pain, in sickness or health; and forsaking all others, to cleave to him only, so long as you both live?"

Answer: I do.

Minister: You will loose your hands.

Exchange of Rings: *The minister will say to the couple,* What pledge have you for the faithful fulfillment of your marriage vows?

Then the man or his attendant at the altar will hand the ring to the minister, who, holding it up so as to be seen, will say:

"This circlet of precious metal is justly regarded as a fitting emblem of the purity and perpetuity of the estate of marriage.

The ancients were reminded by the circle of eternity, as it is so fashioned as to have neither beginning nor end; while gold is so incorruptible that it cannot be tarnished by use or time. So may the union, at this time solemnized, be incorruptible in its purity and more lasting than time itself."

The minister will give the ring to the bridegroom with the following instructions: You will call your name and repeat the following after me: "With this ring, given to thee, as a token of my love, I seal my vows; and with all my earthly possession, I thee endow, in the name of the Father, and of the Son, and of the Holy Spirit. Amen."

If it is a double ring ceremony the bride may repeat the same as did the bridegroom, while placing the ring on the hand of the bridegroom.

Prayer: *The couple will kneel and a soloist will sing* The Wedding Song *as a prayer.*

The Ceremony of the Candles: *Following* The Wedding Song *the couple will rise, taking a lighted candle, and light the unity candle signifying their oneness in marriage.*

Presentation of the Bride and Groom: *Following the lighting of the unity candle, the minister introduces the couple to assembled congregation;*

I now present to you Mr. and Mrs. _____.

Recessional: *The bridal party, led by the bride and groom will exit to appropriate wedding music. This music may include* The Wedding March *or* Joyful, Joyful We Adore Thee.

Wedding Sermon: General
By Robert J. Morgan

Leaving, Cleaving, and Weaving

Dear friends, we are together in this sweet and sacred hour to witness the uniting of _____ and _____ in the enduring bonds of Christian marriage. This happiest and holiest of human relationships was first celebrated in the quiet gardens of Eden, in the springtime of world history. God saw that it was not good for man to live alone, and so He created woman and gave her to him to be his companion, his wife. The Lord said: "Therefore a man shall leave his father and mother and be joined to his wife, and they shall become one flesh."

This first description of marriage gives us three words for the establishing of a home. The first is leaving. "Therefore a man shall leave his father and mother." When a man and a woman establish a new home, there is a sense in which they leave their old ones. They don't leave in terms of love or communication. But they leave in terms of authority and priority. The most important human relationship for you now is the one you're establishing today, in this place and before these witnesses. The primary relationship in your life shifts from the parental to the spousal, from mother and father to husband and wife.

The second idea in Genesis 2:24 is cleaving. "Therefore a man shall leave his father and mother and be joined, be united, shall cleave, to his wife." The word "cleave" means to stick like glue, to be devoted, committed to each other. Every marriage goes through difficult periods and challenging times. It's easy for love to grow lukewarm, then cold. Disillusionment can descend on a home like a Smokey

Mountain fog. That's why you have to remember that divorce is never an option, that the vows you are taking before God are holy, binding, and permanent. You are today deciding to stick to one another like glue, through thick and thin, through good and bad.

We know not what the encircling years will bring, nor how life and labor will unfold before you. But whatever the passing seasons hold, you must always remember to keep your poise, guard your purity, find your place, and fulfill your purpose. *Do all things without complaining and disputing, that you may become blameless and harmless, children of God without fault in the midst of a crooked and perverse generation, among whom you shine as lights in the world (Philippians 2:14–15).*

But that leads to a third concept in Genesis 2:24: Weaving. The verse goes on to say that the man and the woman who leave their parents, cleave to one another, should then become as one. They should weave their lives together. Marriage requires developing common interests, common hobbies, good communication, time together, frequent dating, and growing love. A wedding takes twenty minutes to perform. A friendship takes a lifetime to perfect.

In your marriage, ". . . walk worthy of the calling with which you were called, with all lowliness and gentleness, with longsuffering, bearing with one another in love, endeavoring to keep the unity of the Spirit in the bond of peace" (Ephesians 4:1–3). And in your marriage, ". . . putting away lying, 'Let each one of you speak truth with his neighbor,'" for we are members of one another. 'Be angry, and do not sin': do not let the sun go down on your wrath, nor give place to the devil. Let no corrupt word proceed out of your mouth, but what is good for necessary edification, that it may impart grace to the hearers" (Ephesians 4:25–27, 29).

In your marriage, "Let all bitterness, wrath, anger, clamor, and evil speaking be put away from you, with all malice. And be kind to one another, tenderhearted, forgiving one another, even as God in Christ forgave you" (Ephesians 4:31–32).

In three words, a godly marriage requires leaving, cleaving, and weaving.

If you then, _____ and _____, having freely and deliberately and prayerfully chosen each other as partners for life, will you please unite your right hands and repeat after me:

In taking the woman I hold by the right hand to be my wedded wife, before God and these witnesses I promise to love her, to honor her in this relationship; and leaving all others to be in all things a true and faithful husband as long as we both shall live.

In taking the man I hold by the right hand to be my wedded husband, before God and these witnesses I promise to love him, to honor him in this relationship; and leaving all others to be in all things a true and faithful wife as long as we both shall live.

Then you are each given to the other for richer or poorer, for better or worse, in sickness and in health by the grace of the Lord Jesus Christ.

Wedding Sermon: For a Second Marriage
By Rev. Todd Kinde

Scripture: Ephesians 5:25–27

Husbands, love your wives, just as Christ also loved the church and gave Himself for her, that He might sanctify and cleanse her with the washing of water by the word, that He might present her to Himself a glorious church, not having spot or wrinkle or any such thing, but that she should be holy and without blemish.

Introduction: As we gather to this ceremony of marriage we must recognize that we come to a Christian wedding. It is not like any other that the world may perform. Yes, the external things look the same. Christian marriage, however, is much different. Its foundation is Christ Jesus our Lord. It is with this foundation in place then that we come to understand the reality of marriage. The truth of Christ's love for His Bride, the Church, must work into our daily situations and relationships. We come today to honor the husband and wife relationship. Marriage is a covenant made between two people to love and loyalty. These two people stand before us to make such a covenant. They come to this new relationship with eyes wide open acknowledging the hard work demanded in committing to exclusive love and loyalty.

Marriage is certainly for our pleasure, enjoyment, and companionship. Marriage, however, is the work of the Living Triune God revealing Himself to humankind. The union between man and woman in marriage is more than sociological or biological. It is theological. The intimacy a man and woman share in marriage is an example, an object lesson, teaching us about an even greater intimacy that Christ has with His bride, the church.

Understanding this dynamic, Paul then uses the Person and work of Christ as a pattern for marriage. Paul addresses the husband in verse 25, charging him to love his wife. Similarly Paul addresses the wife in verse 33, charging her to respect her husband. We see mutual interplay between husband and wife to love and respect one another within the covenant of marriage. What is the nature of this love and respect that has been renewed, rediscovered, and rekindled in the hearts of these two people today?

1. Love Gives (Ephesians 5:25). As Christ loved the church and gave himself up for her, so too love and respect within marriage give. Christ so loved that He gave Himself for His church. This kind of love is unconditional. It loves for better or worse, for richer or poorer, in sickness and in health. This love chases after the one who is hurting and weak. This love gives where the other person is not able to give. This love is concerned about pleasing the other.

There are no strings attached to this love. This love has given up all rights to self and flows freely in gracious generosity. Love gives special gifts—not necessarily expensive gifts or many gifts, but small thoughtful tokens of love and respect. Love gives in serving one another. Love gives in exclusive time together. Love gives in a gentle touch. Love gives in tender words.

2. Love Cleanses (Ephesians 5:26). As Christ sanctifies and cleanses the church, so too love and respect within marriage cleanse and purify. The bride and the groom have been preparing themselves for this ceremony. They have taken time washing, shaving, gargling, perfuming and cologning, dressing in a beautiful gown and dapper tuxedo. Because they love one another they clean up for one other.

But the cleansing is more than just what we see on the surface. There is an inner spiritual cleansing that has occurred and will continue throughout this new relationship. Verse 25 tells us that Jesus cleanses His bride, the church, through the washing of the Word. Have you thought about the Scriptures in that way? When you come to read the Scriptures you are in actuality soaking in a spiritual bath. Jesus cleans you by washing you with His Word.

In a marriage relationship, any marriage relationship, we come with some residue that needs to be washed. The Word of God makes us new. The joy and delight a husband and wife share is to come daily to the Word of God and apply the sponge of His love to the areas in our spirit that need cleansed. Love is unconditional and accepts us as we are, but true love loves deeply enough not to leave us as we are.

3. Love Exalts (Ephesians 5:27). As Christ will exalt His bride, the church, to present her pure and holy, so too love and respect within marriage will lift and exalt one another. Christ prepares His church to present her to Himself in the royal sanctuary. He lifts her out from her humble place and exalts her. Psalm 45:13–15 gives us this picture,

> The royal daughter is all glorious within the palace;
> Her clothing is woven with gold.
> She shall be brought to the King in robes of many
>   colors;
> The virgins, her companions who follow her, shall be
>   brought to You.
> With gladness and rejoicing they shall be brought;
> They shall enter the King's palace.

This psalm which pictures the royal wedding of Israel's king and the raising of his bride to enter the palace is also a picture of the work of Christ for His bride. He will lift us to His royal dwelling. Love that gives and cleanses, exalts.

In another place Paul says, "Therefore comfort each other and edify one another, just as you also are doing" (1 Thessalonians 5:11). To be loved and to love is a great lifting experience. A husband and wife in love free each other to greater heights of fulfillment and strength. Walk together climbing the hills of life as you gently encourage one another to the exalted height of true love and fellowship.

Conclusion: It is this kind of love that has been rediscovered here today. Love that gives, cleanses and exalts. We cannot do this in and of ourselves. We must be changed by the power of God through faith in Christ who gave himself for us. Then God takes residence in us. It is only then that you will find the life, love and respect you are seeking. We become the temple of God and by the controlling and enabling of His Holy Spirit we can love, honor, and cherish from this day forward and forever.

Wedding Sermon: Informal/Home
By Robert J. Morgan

A Wedding from 1 John 1:7

Dear friends: We are gathered here in the presence of God and these witnesses to unite this couple in holy marriage. _____ and _____, the two of you are embarking upon an adventurous voyage across the restless sea of the rest of life. You're standing now at the helm of a home about to be launched. The water here in the bay is calm, but soon, within days and months, the winds will blow harder and the waves will curl higher. As you plow the deep, you'll pass over the watery graves of millions of sunken ships of marriages that were overcome by the billows, smashed by the rocks, and confused in the storms by defective compasses.

Today (Tonight) I'm going to give you a compass that works. It has two points, and if both of you keep both of these points aligned, you'll surely and safely arrive at the heavenly harbor together at the end of your earthly voyage. The two compass points are two simple instructions based on a verse of Scripture: 1 John 1:7, "But if we walk in the light as He is in the light, we have fellowship with one another, and the blood of Jesus Christ His Son cleanses us from all sin."

The first needle of direction is this: Walk with the Master. The second compass point is: Work on the marriage. One of these without the other is as useless to your union as one of you without the other. But both of them aligned in both your lives will provide accurate navigation even in the wildest typhoons. Walk with the Master, and work on the marriage.

The reason I can give you this golden compass with such confidence is because, based as it is upon 1 John 1:7, it comes straight from the Lord Himself who said in that verse: If we walk in the light of His presence, we will have fellowship with one another and the blood of Jesus Christ cleanses us from all sin.

Now if this ship that we are launching today (tonight) on the sea of matrimony is the fellowSHIP of 1 John 1:7, Jesus Christ will be the captain, and the relationSHIP will be a godly partnerSHIP, not a godless battleSHIP.

It will sail on, when the soft winds of pleasant days blow across it.

It will sail on, when the whirlpools of financial hardship swirl around it.

It will sail on, when the bright clouds of parental responsibility drift above it.

It will sail on, when the billows of misunderstanding, sickness, tragedy, and death crash against it.

It will sail on because it will be steered by Jesus Christ, blown on its way by the winds of the Holy Spirit, steadied by the anchors of daily Bible study, prayer, and regular church attendance. And it will be loaded with the priceless cargo of that biblical sort of love that does so much, remains so constant, forgives so frequently, acts so sensitively.

The Bible teaches us to let our hearts be knit together in love. There will be times when it will seem easier to quit than to knit—but it's not. Just keep on knitting your hearts together, committing yourselves to Christ, submitting yourselves to each other, omitting the black curse of bad habits from your home, and emitting the fruit of the Spirit in the context of a godly family life.

This is God's plan for you—His fellowship of love and excitement for all those who walk with the Master and work on the marriage.

If you, then _____ and _____ have freely and deliberately chosen each other as partners in this holy estate, and know of no just cause why you should not be so united, in token thereof, will you please join your right hands.

_____, will you repeat after me: *In taking the woman I hold by the right hand to be my wedded wife, before God and these witnesses I promise to love her, to honor her and cherish her in this relationship, and leaving all others, cleave only unto her, in all things a true and faithful husband, as long as we both shall live.*

_____, will you repeat after me: *In taking the man I hold by the right hand to be my wedded husband, before God and these witnesses I promise to love him, to honor him and cherish him in this relationship, and leaving all others, cleave only unto him, in all things a true and faithful wife, as long as we both shall live.*

Then you are each given to the other for richer or poorer, for better or worse, in sickness and in health, till death shall you part.

The wedding ring is a fitting symbol of these vows in two ways. The shape of the ring reminds us that marriage is a never-ending relationship which grows ever sweeter through the ever-encircling years. And the gold gives us a lesson about the glory and the purity of the home.

_____, will you please place the ring on _____ finger and repeat after me: *With this ring I thee wed, with love and joy, through the grace of the Father, and of the Son, and of the Holy Spirit.*

_____, will you please place the ring on _____ finger and repeat after me: *With this ring I thee wed, with love and joy, through the grace of the Father, and of the Son, and of the Holy Spirit.*

Now, upon your mutual promise, made in the presence of God and these witnesses, and according to the authority invested in me as a minister of the gospel of Jesus Christ, I pronounce you husband and wife.

Vow Renewal Ceremony
By Rev. Mark Hollis

A Sample Order of Service for a Vow Renewal Ceremony

Prelude

Processional

Welcome

Prayer

Musical Selection

Scripture

Declaration of Intent

Renewal Homily

Renewal of Vows

Communion

Lighting of Unity Candle

Musical Selection

Prayer of Dedication

Presentation

Recessional

A Sample Detailed Vow Renewal Ceremony

Prelude: *This may be a traditional wedding song or a special song chosen by the couple.*

Processional: *The processional usually only made up of the husband and wife. Often, vow renewal ceremonies are casual and small.*

Welcome: On behalf of _____ and _____, I want to welcome all of you to this special ceremony. This is a happy occasion and a special opportunity to be among God's people. It is appropriate that we seek the Lord's presence as we gather on this special occasion.

Prayer: Father, You have created us for one another. It is with great joy that we join together this evening as _____ and _____ renew their vows before you and this company. We know that you are already present with us. We ask that we would especially sense your presence. We are you children. We thank you for honoring us with your presence this evening. Amen.

The congregation is seated.

Musical Selection: *A song from the couple's wedding or another appropriate selection may be sung.*

Scripture: "Therefore, as the elect of God, holy and beloved, put on tender mercies, kindness, humility, meekness, longsuffering; bearing with one another, and forgiving one another, if anyone has a complaint against another; even as Christ forgave you, so you also must do. But above all these things put on love, which is the bond of perfection. And let the peace of God rule in your hearts, to which also you were called in one body; and be thankful. Let the word of Christ dwell in you richly in all wisdom, teaching and admonishing one another in psalms and hymns and spiritual songs, singing with grace in your hearts to the Lord. And whatever you do in word or deed, do all in the name of the Lord Jesus, giving thanks to God the Father through Him. Wives, submit to your own husbands, as is fitting in the Lord. Husbands, love your wives and do not be bitter toward them" (Colossians 3:12–19).

"Love suffers long and is kind; love does not envy; love does not parade itself, is not puffed up; does not behave rudely, does not seek its own, is not provoked, thinks no evil; does not rejoice in iniquity, but rejoices in the truth; bears all things, believes all things, hopes all things, endures all things. Love never fails . . ." (1 Corinthians 13:4–8).

Declaration of Intent: _____ (husband), understanding that this is God's instruction to you regarding how you are to love _____ (wife), as the Holy Spirit empowers you, do you recommit yourself to love her in this way? Do you promise to love and uphold her and to join with her in making a home that shall endure in love and in peace? Do you reaffirm your commitment to a deeper union with her whereby you shall both know joy and fulfillment of love? Do you renew your pledge to complete faithfulness through all the changing seasons of life? Do you now, of your own free will, give yourself completely to her to love her in body, mind, and soul that you shall be hers alone as long as you both shall live?

Husband: I do.

_____ (wife), understanding that this is God's instruction to you regarding how you are to love _____ (husband), as the Holy Spirit empowers you, do you recommit yourself to love him in this way? Do you promise to love and uphold him and to join with him in making a home that shall endure in love and in peace? Do you reaffirm your commitment to a deeper union with him whereby you shall both know joy and fulfillment of love? Do you renew your pledge to complete faithfulness through all the changing seasons of life? Do you now, of your own free will, give yourself completely to him to love him in body, mind, and soul that you shall be his alone as long as you both shall live?

Wife: I do.

Renewal Homily: I encourage you to listen to the words of Scripture. Make mercy, kindness, humility, meekness, and patience the regular practice of your regular days. Put them on like a garment each morning and never take them off throughout the day. These are the practical edges of love. They are the tools that allow us to live together in harmony.

". . . Bearing with one another, and forgiving one another . . ." (Colossians 3:13). Forgiveness is a key element in keeping your marriage healthy. It unlocks the door to the heart grown cold. It frees us from bitterness and allows us to love regardless of the faults of the other.

"Let the word of Christ dwell in you richly" (Colossians 3:16). Love is not something that comes from outside of us. It cannot be bought or sold. It is not a commodity. Love comes from within us. It is sometimes a feeling, but more often a choice. It is a spiritual presence. It is God fitting us in a special dimension and enabling us to love through His power. All of the virtues of love, patience, kindness, forgiveness, compassion, gentleness, humility, and peace flow naturally out of the presence of the Holy Spirit in our lives. As we yield ourselves to Him, He lives His life through us. As we depend on Him, these virtues actually become a part of our own spirit.

You have had the opportunity to live together for many years. Your love has matured. Your expectations have met with reality and the expectations have had to be adjusted. Through it all you have decided to persevere. At some point in your life you have each had the opportunity to acknowledge Christ as your Savior. He gave His life for you and now He gives His life to you. He is committed to your marriage. You are flawed and weak. His Spirit makes your love vibrant and strong.

Renewal of Vows: Think back to that day when you first pledged your love to each other. Your love was young and strong. You had grand dreams and a bright future. Now you have reached a new plateau in your life. You have faced the challenges of children, mortgages, and bills. You have seen the changes that come with the years. Still you are committed to one another and are giving public testimony to that commitment in this service.

As you renew your vows you can make these promises with boldness. Your love is more mature and refined than it was. The challenges have been real, but God has been with you. He is with us today as well. He stands as a witness to these vows. He stands ready to help you fulfill them, so repeat your vows with boldness.

_____ (husband), looking at your wife and taking her right hand in yours, repeat after me.

I renew now the vows I made when we became husband and wife. I _____ (husband's full name), take you _____ (wife's full name) to be my wife, to have and to hold from this day forward, for better for worse, for richer for poorer, in sickness and in health, to love and to cherish, until we are parted by death. This is my solemn vow.

_____ (wife), looking at your husband and taking his right hand in yours, repeat after me.

I renew now the vows I made when we became husband and wife. I _____ (wife's full name), take you _____ (husband's full name) to be my husband, to have and to hold from this day forward, for better for worse, for richer for poorer, in sickness and in health, to love and to cherish, until we are parted by death. This is my solemn vow.

Communion: At the final Passover meal Jesus shared with His disciples He got up from the meal to wash His disciples' feet. He took bread and breaking it gave it to His disciples, saying,

"Take, eat; this is My body" (Mark 14:22).

He then took the cup and offered it to His disciples saying,

"This is My blood of the new covenant, which is shed for many" (Mark 14:24).

_____ (husband),
_____ (wife), it is because of His sacrifice that the two of you stand redeemed before Him today. It is only in Jesus that your marriage can become all that you and God want it to be. It is only in His goodness and power that you can keep your vows to one another.

Since that night more than 2,000 years ago Christian leaders have led their flocks, small and large, in remembering the Lord's sacrifice on their behalf by celebrating the Lord's Table or communion together. As a couple you celebrate communion together on this special day. _____ (husband), as the spiritual leader in your home, I invite you to come and serve your wife remembering the sacrifice of Christ on your behalf.

Husband and wife come to the table where husband serves wife and they partake of communion together.

Lighting of Unity Candle: *The couple steps to the table where unity candle has been placed with one single candle at each end and one larger candle in the middle. Husband and wife each take a candle and together light the center candle then extinguishing the flame of their own candles.*

Musical Selection: *The Lord's Prayer or another musical selection may be sung at this time.*

Prayer of Dedication: Father, we look to you as the source for every good thing in our life. Some years ago you looked down as these two pledged their love and commitment to one another. You have watched and participated as their love has grown and as their journey through life has continued. We look to you now for continued and renewed blessings on them. Give them good spirits and renewed love for one another. I ask that the fruit of the Spirit would be evident in their lives. Give them a love, which is their life. Give them a love, which is beyond their natural ability to love – a love, which comes from You. Give them Your peace and confidence that You are committed to their marriage. Give them the simple ability to be gracious to one another. Grant them the gift of faithfulness. Give them gentleness and self-control. Bring a new joy to their marriage. Allow each to be confident in the love of the other. Give them the freedom to love as You have loved them. Thank You, Father, that You have given us the gift of Yourself.

Presentation: _____ and
_____ have renewed their vows to one another and have sealed their commitment through prayer and the giving and receiving of communion. Now I present them to you. Will you commit yourselves to uphold them before the Lord in prayer? Stand as a symbol of that commitment.

Depending on the couple's preference, they may wish to kiss at this point.

Recessional: *Depending on the size of the congregation and personal preference, the couple will decide whether or not to have a recessional.*

Traditional Wedding Scriptures

Genesis 1:28: Then God blessed them, and God said to them, "Be fruitful and multiply; fill the earth and subdue it; have dominion over the fish of the sea, over the birds of the air, and over every living thing that moves on the earth."

Genesis 2:18–24: And the LORD God said, "It is not good that man should be alone; I will make him a helper comparable to him." Out of the ground the LORD God formed every beast of the field and every bird of the air, and brought them to Adam to see what he would call them. And whatever Adam called each living creature, that was its name. So Adam gave names to all cattle, to the birds of the air, and to every beast of the field. But for Adam there was not found a helper comparable to him. And the Lord God caused a deep sleep to fall on Adam, and he slept; and He took one of his ribs, and closed up the flesh in its place. Then the rib which the LORD God had taken from man He made into a woman, and He brought her to the man. And Adam said: "This is now bone of my bones and flesh of my flesh; she shall be called Woman, because she was taken out of Man." Therefore a man shall leave his father and mother and be joined to his wife, and they shall become one flesh.

Ruth 1:16–17: "Entreat me not to leave you, or to turn back from following after you; for wherever you go, I will go; and wherever you lodge, I will lodge; your people shall be my people, and your God, my God. Where you die, I will die, and there will I be buried. The Lord do so to me, and more also, if anything but death parts you and me."

Psalm 127:1: Unless the LORD builds the house, they labor in vain who build it; unless the Lord guards the city, the watchman stays awake in vain.

Psalm 128:1–4: Blessed is every one who fears the LORD, who walks in His ways. When you eat the labor of your hands, you shall be happy, and it shall be well with you. Your wife shall be like a fruitful vine in the very heart of your house, your children like olive plants all around your table. Behold, thus shall the man be blessed who fears the LORD.

Ecclesiastes 4:9–12: Two are better than one, because they have a good reward for their labor. For if they fall, one will lift up his companion. But woe to him who is alone when he falls, for he has no one to help him up. Again, if two lie down together, they will keep warm; but how can one be warm alone? Though one may be overpowered by another, two can withstand him. And a threefold cord is not quickly broken.

Song of Solomon 2:10–14, 16: My beloved spoke, and said to me: "Rise up, my love, my fair one, and come away. For lo, the winter is past, the rain is over and gone. The flowers appear on the earth; the time of singing has come, and the voice of the turtledove is heard in our land. The fig tree puts forth her green figs, and the vines with the tender grapes give a good smell. Rise up, my love, my fair one, and come away! O my dove, in the clefts of the rock, in the secret places of the cliff, let me see your face, let me hear your voice; for your voice is sweet, and your face is lovely." . . . My beloved is mine, and I am his.

Song of Solomon 8:6–7: Set me as a seal upon your heart, as a seal upon your arm; for love is as strong as death, jealousy as cruel as the grave; its flames are flames of fire, a most vehement flame. Many waters cannot quench love, nor can the floods drown it . . .

Isaiah 26:3–4: You will keep him in perfect peace, whose mind is stayed on You, because he trusts in You. Trust in the LORD forever, for in Yah, the LORD, is everlasting strength.

Matthew 22:37–40: "Jesus said to him, 'You shall love the LORD your God with all your heart, with all your soul, and with all your mind.' This is the first and great commandment. And the second is like it: 'You shall love your neighbor as yourself.' On these two commandments hang all the Law and the Prophets."

Mark 10:6–9: "But from the beginning of the creation, God 'made them male and female.' 'For this reason a man shall leave his father and mother and be joined to his wife, and the two shall become one flesh'; so then they are no longer two, but one flesh. Therefore what God has joined together, let not man separate."

Mark 10:42–45: But Jesus called them to Himself and said to them, "You know that those who are considered rulers over the Gentiles lord it over them, and their great ones exercise authority over them. Yet it shall not be so among you; but whoever desires to become great among you shall be your servant. And whoever of you desires to be first shall be slave of all. For even the Son of Man did not come to be served, but to serve, and to give His life a ransom for many."

John 2:1–11: On the third day there was a wedding in Cana of Galilee, and the mother of Jesus was there. Now both Jesus and His disciples were invited to the wedding. And when they ran out of wine, the mother of Jesus said to Him, "They have no wine." Jesus said to her, "Woman, what does your concern have to do with Me? My hour has not yet come." His mother said to the servants, "Whatever He says to you, do it." Now there were set there six water-pots of stone, according to the manner of purification of the Jews, containing twenty or thirty gallons apiece. Jesus said to them, "Fill the waterpots with water." And they filled them up to the brim. And He said to them, "Draw some out now, and take it to the master of the feast." And they took it. When the master of the feast had tasted the water that was made wine, and did not know where it came from (but the servants who had drawn the water knew), the master of the feast called the bridegroom. And he said to him, "Every man at the beginning sets out the good wine, and when the guests have well drunk, then the inferior. You have kept the good wine until now!" This beginning of signs Jesus did in Cana of Galilee, and manifested His glory; and His disciples believed in Him.

John 15:9–12: "As the Father loved Me, I also have loved you; abide in My love. If you keep My commandments, you will abide in My love, just as I have kept My Father's commandments and abide in His love. These things I have spoken to you, that My joy may remain in you, and that your joy may be full. This is My commandment, that you love one another as I have loved you."

Romans 12:9–18: Let love be without hypocrisy. Abhor what is evil. Cling to what is good. Be kindly affectionate to one another with brotherly love, in honor giving preference to one another; not lagging in diligence, fervent in spirit, serving the Lord; rejoicing in hope, patient in tribulation, continuing steadfastly in prayer; distributing to the needs of the saints, given to hospitality. Bless those who persecute you; bless and do not curse. Rejoice with those who rejoice, and weep with those who weep. Be of the same mind toward one another. Do not set your mind on high things, but associate with the humble. Do not be wise in your own opinion. Repay no one evil for evil. Have regard for good things in the sight of all men. If it is possible, as much as depends on you, live peaceably with all men.

1 Corinthians 13:4–7: Love suffers long and is kind; love does not envy; love does not parade itself, is not puffed up; does not behave rudely, does not seek its own, is not provoked, thinks no evil; does not rejoice in iniquity, but rejoices in the truth; bears all things, believes all things, hopes all things, endures all things.

1 Corinthians 16:14: Let all that you do be done with love.

Ephesians 4:25–32: Therefore, putting away lying, "Let each one of you speak truth with his neighbor," for we are members of one another. "Be angry, and do not sin": do not let the sun go down on your wrath, nor give place to the devil. Let him who stole steal no longer, but rather let him labor, working with his hands what is good, that he may have something to give him who has need. Let no corrupt word proceed out of your mouth, but what is good for necessary edification, that it may impart grace to the hearers. And do not grieve the Holy Spirit of God, by whom you were sealed for the day of redemption. Let all bitterness, wrath, anger, clamor, and evil speaking be put away from you, with all malice. And be kind to one another, tender-hearted, forgiving one another, even as God in Christ forgave you.

Ephesians 5:22–33: Wives, submit to your own husbands, as to the Lord. For the husband is head of the wife, as also Christ is head of the church; and He is the Savior of the body. Therefore, just as the church is subject to Christ, so let the wives be to their own husbands in everything. Husbands, love your wives, just as Christ also loved the church and gave Himself for her, that He might sanctify and cleanse her with the washing of water by the word, that He might present her to Himself a glorious church, not having spot or wrinkle or any such thing, but that she should be holy and without blemish. So husbands ought to love their own wives as their own bodies; he who loves his wife loves himself. For no one ever hated his own flesh, but nourishes and cherishes it, just as the Lord does the church. For we are members of His body, of His flesh and of His bones. "For this reason a man shall leave his father and mother and be joined to his wife, and the two shall become one flesh." This is a great mystery, but I speak concerning Christ and the church. Nevertheless let each one of you in particular so love his own wife as himself, and let the wife see that she respects her husband.

Philippians 2:1–11: Therefore if there is any consolation in Christ, if any comfort of love, if any fellowship of the Spirit, if any affection and mercy, fulfill my joy by being like-minded, having the same love, being of one accord, of one mind. Let nothing be done through selfish ambition or conceit, but in lowliness of mind let each esteem others better than himself. Let each of you look out not only for his own interests, but also for the interests of others. Let this mind be in you which was also in Christ Jesus, who, being in the form of God, did not consider it robbery to be equal with God, but made Himself of no reputation, taking the form of a bondservant, and coming in the likeness of men. And being found in appearance as a man, He humbled Himself and became obedient to the point of death, even the death of the cross. Therefore God also has highly exalted Him and given Him the name which is above every name, that at the name of Jesus every knee should bow, of those in heaven, and of those on earth, and of those under the earth, and that every tongue should confess that Jesus Christ is Lord, to the glory of God the Father.

Colossians 3:12–17: Therefore, as the elect of God, holy and beloved, put on tender mercies, kindness, humility, meekness, longsuffering; bearing with one another, and forgiving one another, if anyone has a complaint against another; even as Christ forgave you, so you also must do. But above all these things put on love, which is the bond of perfection. And let the peace of God rule in your hearts, to which also you were called in one body; and be thankful. Let the word of Christ dwell in you richly in all wisdom, teaching and admonishing one another in psalms and hymns and spiritual songs, singing with grace in your hearts to the Lord. And whatever you do in word or deed, do all in the name of the Lord Jesus, giving thanks to God the Father through Him.

Colossians 3:18–19: Wives, submit to your own husbands, as is fitting in the Lord. Husbands, love your wives and do not be bitter toward them.

1 John 4:7–11: Beloved, let us love one another, for love is of God; and everyone who loves is born of God and knows God. He who does not love does not know God, for God is love. In this the love of God was manifested toward us, that God has sent His only begotten Son into the world, that we might live through Him. In this is love, not that we loved God, but that He loved us and sent His Son to be the propitiation for our sins. Beloved, if God so loved us, we also ought to love one another.

Favorite Wedding Hymns
By Jerry Carraway

Cherish the Treasure, Jon Mohr; © 1988 Jonathan Mark Music/Birdwing Music (Admin. by EMI Christian Music Publishing.)

Household of Faith, Brent Lamb/John Rosasco; © 1983 Straightway Music (Admin. by EMI Christian Music Publishing.)

I Will Be Here, Steven Curtis Champman; © 1989, 1990 Greg Nelson Music/Careers-BMG Music Publishing (Admin. by EMI Christian Music Publishing.)

Joyful, Joyful We Adore Thee, Henry Van Dyke/Ludwig van Beethoven; Public Domain.

Somewhere in the World, Wayne Watson; © 1985 Word Music, Inc.

When Love Is Found, Brian Wren; © 1983 Hope Publishing Company.

Love Divine, All Loves Excelling, Charles Wesley/John Zundel; Public Domain.

O Perfect Love, Dorothy F. Gurney; Public Domain.

Savior, Like a Shepherd Lead Us, Dorothy A. Thrupp/William B. Bradbury; Public Domain.

Rejoice, Ye Pure in Heart, Edward H. Plumptre; Public Domain.

The King of Love My Shepherd Is, Henry W. Baker/John B. Dykes; Public Domain.

Funerals

Funeral Registration Form

Name: _____

Age: _____

Brief Bio: _____

_____

_____

_____

Name of Spouse: _____

Name of Parents: _____

and _____

Names of Children: _____

_____

Names of Siblings: _____

_____

Names of Grandchildren: _____

_____

Funeral Home: _____

Time and Place of Visitation: _____

Time and Place of Funeral: _____

Minister Officiating: _____

Time and Place of Graveside Service: _____

Pallbearers: _____

_____

Burial Site: _____

Family Preferences: _____

_____

_____

Sample Funeral Service
By Dr. Melvin Worthington

A Sample Funeral Order of Service

Prelude   *Special Music*

Hymn   *Sermon*

Scripture Reading   *Benediction*

Prayer

A Sample Detailed Funeral Service

This order of service is for a funeral at the home, funeral home chapel, or a church. The minister must keep in mind that the funeral service affords an excellent opportunity for biblical instruction.

Prelude: *The organist or pianist should play appropriate music. Hymns might include* Safe in the Arms of Jesus, The Old Rugged Cross, Beyond the Sunset, Amazing Grace, It Is Well With My Soul, *and* Abide With Me. *The minister should to check with the family and see if the deceased had any favorite hymns that could be used at this point.*

Hymn: *Sung by choir, soloist, congregation, or selected group.*

Scripture Reading: The Lord is my shepherd; I shall not want. He makes me to lie down in green pastures; He leads me beside the still waters. He restores my soul; He leads me in the paths of righteousness for His name's sake. Yea, though I walk through the valley of the shadow of death, I will fear no evil; for You are with me; Your rod and Your staff, they comfort me. You prepare a table before me in the presence of my enemies; You anoint my head with oil; my cup runs over. Surely goodness and mercy shall follow me all the days of my life; and I will dwell in the house of the LORD forever (Psalm 23).

"LORD, make me to know my end, and what is the measure of my days, that I may know how frail I am. Indeed, You have made my days as handbreadths, and my age is as nothing before You; certainly every man at his best state is but vapor. Selah. Surely every man walks about like a shadow; surely they busy themselves in vain; he heaps up riches, and does not know who will gather them. And now, Lord, what do I wait for? My hope is in You. Deliver me from all my transgressions; do not make me the reproach of the foolish. I was mute, I did not open my mouth, because it was You who did it. Remove Your plague from me; I am consumed by the blow of Your hand. When with rebukes You correct man for iniquity, You make his beauty melt away like a moth; surely every man is vapor. Selah. "Hear my prayer, O LORD, and give ear to my cry; do not be silent at my tears; for I am a stranger with You, a sojourner, as all my fathers were. Remove Your gaze from me, that I may regain strength, before I go away and am no more" (Psalm 39:4–13).

"Let not your heart be troubled; you believe in God, believe also in Me. In my Father's house are many mansions; if it were not so, I would have told you. I go to prepare a place for you. And if I go and prepare a place for you, I will come again and receive you to Myself; that where I am, there you may be also. And where I go you know, and the way you know." Thomas said to Him, "Lord, we do not know where You are going, and how can we know the way?" Jesus said to him, "I am the way, the truth, and the life. No one comes to the Father except through me" (John 14:1–6).

But I do not want you to be ignorant, brethren, concerning those who have fallen asleep, lest you sorrow as others who have not hope. For if we believe that Jesus died and rose again, even so God will bring with Him those who sleep in Jesus. For this we say to you by the word of the Lord, that we who are alive and remain until the coming of the Lord will by no means precede those who are asleep. For the Lord Himself will descend from heaven with a shout, with the voice of an archangel, and with the trumpet of God. And the dead in Christ will rise first. Then we who are alive and remain shall be caught up together with them in the clouds to meet the Lord in the air. And thus we shall always be with the Lord. Therefore comfort one another with these words (1 Thessalonians 4:13–18).

Prayer: Oh, Lord, You fashioned us while we were yet in our mothers' womb. You have provided for us, and You have guided us through this journey of life. Now we are faced with the reality of death, for our loved one has come to the end of life. So, even now, we put our trust in You. Give us comfort in our sorrow. Help us to focus on You, on the eternity You offer when we follow You. In Jesus' name we pray these things, Amen.

Hymn: *Sung by a choir, soloist, duet, selected group, or the congregation.*

Special Music: *Sung by choir, selected group, or soloist. This music could be selected by the family.*

Sermon: *For help with the funeral sermon, see the sample outlines following this order of service.*

Benediction: Now this I say, brethren, that flesh and blood cannot inherit the kingdom of God; nor does corruption inherit incorruption. Behold, I tell you a mystery: We shall not all sleep, but we shall all be changed—in a moment, in the twinkling of an eye, at the last trumpet. For the trumpet will sound, and the dead will be raised incorruptible, and we shall be changed. For this corruptible must put on incorruption, and this mortal must put on immortality. So when this corruptible has put on incorruption, and this mortal has put on immortality, then shall be brought to pass the saying that is written: "Death is swallowed up in victory." "O Death, where is your sting? O Hades, where is your victory?" The sting of death is sin, and the strength of sin is the law. But thanks be to God, who gives us the victory through out Lord Jesus Christ. Therefore, my beloved brethren, be steadfast, immovable, always abounding in the work of the Lord, knowing that your labor is not in vain in the Lord (1 Corinthians 15:50–58).

When the service is to be concluded at the graveside, the benediction may be omitted until the body is deposited in the grave. At the graveside, appropriate Scripture is read and the benediction is given. See the sample graveside services for additional guidance.

Funeral Sermon: General
By Joshua Rowe

Caught Up Together in the Clouds

Today we have gathered in honor and memory of

(Personal Comments)

Scripture: 1 Thessalonians 4:13–18, NASB—But we do not want you to be uninformed, brethren, about those who are asleep, that you may not grieve, as do the rest who have no hope. For if we believe that Jesus died and rose again, even so God will bring with Him those who have fallen asleep in Jesus. For this we say to you by the word of the Lord, that we who are alive and remain until the coming of the Lord, shall not precede those who have fallen asleep. For the Lord Himself will descend from heaven with a shout, with the voice of the archangel, and with the trumpet of God; and the dead in Christ shall rise first. Then we who are alive and remain will be caught up together with them in the clouds to meet the Lord in the air, and thus we shall always be with the Lord. Therefore comfort one another with these words.

Introduction: In this time when we feel such heartache, pain, and loss, Scripture offers us so much comfort, encouragement, and victory. It seems that, in writing to the Thessalonian believers, Paul knew of some church members who recently lost a loved one. To those who are hurting and grieving, he offers reason to hope.

1. **A Different Reaction** (v. 13). Paul specifically addresses those in the church who have lost friends, family, or loved ones. He tells them that we should react differently than those who "have no hope." Two things to keep in mind:

   A. *Our Mourning Is Natural.* Paul is not saying that we should not be sad when our loved ones die. Psalm 116:15 is often translated, "Precious in the sight of the Lord is the death of His godly ones." The Hebrew word for "precious" refers often to precious stones or possessions; it can also be translated "costly, expensive." The Lord does His work on earth through His people, so doesn't it make sense that their death is costly? He knows our loss because He experiences it with us! Do you remember the story about Lazarus' death? Jesus knew that He would raise Lazarus from the dead (John 11:4), but when he saw the sad faces, approached the sealed tomb, and felt the loss of a loved one, Jesus wept (John 11:35). We know that departed believers will be resurrected, but being apart from them causes natural pain and grief.

   B. *Our Rejoicing Is Supernatural.* Paul explains that we are to react differently than those who have no hope. Although we mourn and grieve, the Lord is with us through it all. As believers, we have comfort and hope in the future: we know that our departed loved ones who were fellow believers are now with the Lord (2 Corinthians 5:8). Scripture even calls them blessed: "And I heard a voice from heaven, saying, 'Write, "Blessed are the dead who die in the Lord from now on!" 'Yes,' says the Spirit, 'that they may rest from their labors, for their deeds follow with them'" (Revelation 14:13, NASB).

2. **An Important Reality** (vv. 14–17). Paul reminds us that if we believe in the gospel, we also believe in the Second Coming of Christ! No topic is more comforting to us in our loss than that of the resurrection; it's the true hope that only we as Christians have. The scene he describes causes us to pause in our grief to anticipate the future:

A. *The Privilege of Deceased Saints* (vv. 14–15). When Christ returns, He will bring the deceased believers with Him! While we grieve their loss, surely they rejoice and anticipate the day when they will be the first to see the resurrected Christ return for His people.

B. *The Triumphant Return of Christ* (v. 16). We are told that, ". . . the Lord Himself will descend from heaven with a shout, with the voice of an archangel, and with the trumpet of God; and the dead in Christ shall rise first" (v. 16). When Christ comes for the second time, it will not be in a manger, wrapped in swaddling clothes, announced by a single star to wise men or by an angel to shepherds; He will come wrapped in glory and splendor with an earth-shaking shout of an archangel, and with the trumpet of God Himself! And who will be the first to see these things? The dead in Christ.

C. *The Triumphant Reunion* (v. 17). After the deceased saints are resurrected to be with Christ in His glory, "Then we who are alive and remain shall be caught up together with them in the clouds to meet the Lord in the air, and thus we shall always be with the Lord" (v. 17). We will be reunited with our fellow believers whom we have lost, and all together we will be united with Christ in all His glory for the rest of eternity!

Conclusion: Today we are naturally grieved. But we also have reason for great comfort. I encourage you to put a bookmark in 1 Thessalonians 4. When you feel the deepest pain, you can read this passage; surely this will engage you in the deepest anticipation of Christ's return. Paul said about these verses, "Therefore comfort one another with these words" (v. 18). As we leave today, let's remind each other in our grief that our friend will be of the first to see the magnificent return of the Savior, Jesus Christ; we shall one day see our friend again, together in the clouds.

Benediction: "Blessed are those who mourn, for they shall be comforted" (Matthew 5:4).

Funeral Sermon: Child or Youth
By Rev. Richard Sharpe

Precious Loss

Today we have gathered in honor and memory of

_____

(Personal Comments)

Scripture: 2 Kings 4:8–37

Introduction: Some years ago we had a set of twins born into our family. One of them had some problems, so after a few weeks of keeping our child, the doctor sent him home with us, giving us "danger signs" to watch for. Unfortunately, the doctor told us to watch for the wrong signs; our son died after only five weeks on this earth. It was hard to lose our son, but we also knew that the Lord had a reason for his death. In the town where I was ministering was a fire department; its members responded to the emergency call regarding our son. They came well equipped to save lives, but they didn't have the equipment to save our son. Everything they had was for an adult. I remember their shock as they stood in our kitchen, unable to help our son. Our son proved to be a witness to the members of the fire department, to their need for the Lord. God has a purpose for everyone coming into this world. Even if it is a short life, there is a reason. In 2 Kings 4 we find a comforting story about the death of a beloved child:

1. A Mother's Wish.—Elisha was a man of God who traveled the country to spread the Word of the Lord. He sometimes needed places to stay in these travels. One particular couple was quite generous, giving him a room to sleep in. This couple had no children. The prophet wanted to do something for the couple; his servant told him that they wanted a child:

> And he said to him, "Say now to her, 'Look, you have been concerned for us with all this care. What can I do for you? Do you want me to speak on your behalf to the king or to the commander of the army?'" She answered, "I dwell among my own people." So he said, "What then is to be done for her?" And Gehazi answered, "Actually, she has no son, and her husband is old." So he said, "Call her." When he had called her, she stood in the doorway. Then he said, "About this time next year you shall embrace a son." And she said, "No, my lord. Man of God, do not lie to your maidservant!" (2 Kings 4:13–16).

She thought he was lying about something that meant so much to her. She knew him to be a man of God but didn't think even God could give her a child at this time in her life.

2. A Mother's Joy.—We read that this woman did have a son when Elisha said she would. Imagine how happy the mother was; imagine how happy his father was to have a hand in the field and a son to be proud of. The child grew older and was going out to help his father in the field. Things seemed to be going so well until one day the child's head started hurting and he was taken into the house with his mother.

3. A Mother's Sorrow.—Not only did her son fall sick but he died. Follow the passage: "And he said to his father, 'My head, my head!' So he said to a servant, 'Carry him to his mother.' When he had taken him and brought him to his mother, he sat on her knees till noon, and then died" (2 Kings

4:19–20). This mother who had so much joy now was beside herself. Her only son was dead. She had to do something. She went to where the man of God was to get his help. She went to Mount Carmel:

> Now when she came to the man of God at the hill, she caught him by the feet, but Gehazi came near to push her away. But the man of God said, "Let her alone; for her soul is in deep distress, and the LORD has hidden it from me, and has not told me." So she said, "Did I ask a son of my lord? Did I not say, 'Do not deceive me'?" Then he said to Gehazi, "Get yourself ready, and take my staff in your hand, and be on your way. If you meet anyone, do not greet him; and if anyone greets you, do not answer him; but lay my staff on the face of the child." And the mother of the child said, "As the LORD lives, and as your soul lives, I will not leave you." So he arose and followed her (2 Kings 4:27–30).

4. A Mother's Hope.—The woman got the prophet's attention and brought him back to the house. The servant, Gehazi, couldn t do anything for the boy except confirm that the child was dead. Elisha attempted to revive the child, but was unsuccessful the first time; listen to the story as it reaches its climax and conclusion:

> He went in therefore, shut the door behind the two of them, and prayed to the LORD. And he went up and lay on the child, and put his mouth on his mouth, his eyes on his eyes, and his hands on his hands; and he stretched himself out on the child, and the flesh of the child became warm. He returned and walked back and forth in the house, and again went up and stretched himself out on him; then the child sneezed seven times, and the child opened his eyes. And he called Gehazi and said, "Call this Shunammite woman." So he called her.

And when she came in to him, he said, "Pick up your son." So she went in, fell at his feet, and bowed to the ground; then she picked up her son and went out (2 Kings 4:33–37).

We find that the son was restored to his mother. It is great to see a child brought back to life. So why *this* story with a happy ending, when our beloved child was not so fortunate? I'm here to share with you the hope that God offers through Jesus Christ. There is a day coming when this child and all his/her friends and loved ones can be reunited with each other. Death does not end life, it begins it. Eternity is in front of us. The Lord is just and righteous to deal with our children; the question is, how will we respond to Him?

Conclusion: Now we as this child's parents or loved ones have a choice to make. We must accept Jesus Christ as our Savior to join this child in heaven. Do you know Christ as your Savior? You can. The Bible has a plan for all those who want to choose Christ. The Bible says in John 3:16: "For God so loved the world that He gave His only begotten Son, that whoever believes in Him should not perish but have everlasting life." Do you believe? Have you turned from your sins and asked Christ to come into your life? You can today. Talk to me after the service. Even in the face of such a difficult situation, God offers us hope through Jesus Christ. Trust in Him and in the promises given to you through the Bible; give Him your heart and let Him ease your pain.

Benediction: "Come to Me, all you who labor and are heavy laden, and I will give you rest. Take My yoke upon you and learn from Me, for I am gentle and lowly in heart, and you will find rest for your souls. For My yoke is easy and My burden is light" (Matthew 11:28–30).

Funeral Sermon:
Accident Victim
By Robert J. Morgan

He Does All Things Well

Today we have gathered in honor and memory of

(Personal Comments)

Scripture: Mark 7:37

"And they were astonished beyond measure, saying, 'He has done all things well'"(Mark 7:37).

Introduction: In these sad moments, we are left feeling lost and devastated. We have so many questions, but the biggest one is "Why?" An old hymn by Anna L. Waring comes to mind today:

In heavenly love abiding, no change my heart shall fear.
And safe in such confiding, for nothing changes here.
The storm may roar without me, my heart may low be laid,
But God is round about me, and can I be dismayed?
Wherever He may guide me, no want shall turn me back.
My Shepherd is beside me, and nothing can I lack.
His wisdom ever waking, His sight is never dim.
He knows the way He's taking, and I will walk with Him.

That phrase, "He knows the way He's taking," is the basis for my remarks today. God knows what He is doing. He doesn't make mistakes, especially of this magnitude. As the people of our Lord's day put it, "He does all things well."

We don't always understand His means or His methods.

He has purposes to which we are not always privy, but we know He does all things well.

His ways are not our ways and His thoughts are not our thoughts, but He does all things well.

He allows winds to blow and storms to rage. Sorrows and tears befall us, and our ways may wend through darkness and difficulty. But as for God, His ways are perfect. He works all things together for good. The Bible says that our times are in His hands.

A. W. Tozer once wrote, "To the child of God, there is no such thing as an accident. He travels an appointed way. Accidents may indeed appear to befall him and misfortune stalk his way, but these evils will be so in appearance only and will seem evils only because we cannot read the secret script of God's hidden providence and so cannot discover the ends at which He aims. . . . The man of true faith may live in the absolute assurance that his steps are ordered by the Lord. For him, misfortune is outside the bounds of possibility. He cannot be torn from this earth one hour ahead of the time which God has appointed, and he cannot be detained on earth one moment after God is done with him here."

He does all things well, and He asks us to trust Him. We can trust Him through sunshine and shadows. When we cannot trace His hand, we can trust His heart.

It is normal, however, to occasionally ask "Why?" Though God may not always answer our "why" questions, He listens to them and responds in the wisest ways.

1. Moses asked: "Lord, why have you brought trouble to this people?"
2. Gideon asked: "Why then has all this happened to us?"
3. Naomi said: "I went out full, and the Lord has brought me home again empty. Why?"
4. Nehemiah asked: "Why is the house of God forsaken?"

5. Job said: "Why have you set me as your target?"
6. David said: "Lord, why do you cast off my soul? Why do You hide Your face from me?"
7. Jeremiah asked: "Why is my pain perpetual and my wound incurable?"

But the greatest "Why" in the Bible was uttered by the Lord Jesus Christ on the Cross when He said, "My God, My God, why have you forsaken me?" And there is something about that "Why" that swallows up all the others.

Because Jesus gave Himself on the Cross, we can trust Him to have answers to all our other "whys."

Vance Havner once said, "You need never ask 'Why?' because Calvary covers it all. When before the throne we stand in Him complete, all the riddles that puzzle us here will fall into place and we shall know in fulfillment what we now believe in faith—that all things work together for good in His eternal purpose. No longer will we cry 'My God, why?' Instead, 'alas' will become 'Alleluia,' all question marks will be straightened into exclamation points, sorrow will change to singing, and pain will be lost in praise."

One thing we do know: The death of a Christian doesn't seem as tragic to God as it does to us. To us it is separation and sorrow. To God it is:

1. A promotion.
2. A release from the burdens of earth.
3. Early furlough from the battle zone.
4. Relocation to a better climate.
5. Instant transport to the celestial city.
6. To depart and be with Christ, which is far better.
7. To be absent from the body but present with the Lord.

Conclusion: Our friend has beaten us to heaven and is more alive than ever, for God is not a God of the dead, but of the living. We don't understand all of God's purposes, but we know He does all things well, and we must simply leave it there, in His love.

Benediction:
In heavenly love abiding, no change my heart shall fear.
And safe in such confiding, for nothing changes here.
The storm may roar without me, my heart may low be laid,
But God is round about me, and can I be dismayed?

Funeral Sermon: Suicide Victim
By Rev. Richard Sharpe

Only One Unpardonable Sin

Today we have gathered in honor and memory of

_____

(Personal Comments)

Scripture: John 3:9–21; 10:25–30

Introduction: One of the main problems we have with this type of tragic death is the fact that we are unsure of what the Bible teaches regarding suicide. Many teach that if someone takes their life they are going to never go to heaven. They say that the individual did not finish well. This leaves family and loved ones in serious doubt and pain. The Bible is very clear about the problem of sin in our world. The Bible teaches that there is only one way to get into heaven, through the Lord Jesus Christ. He died on the cross for the sins of the world. If an individual accepts Christ as their personal Savior, they will be in heaven. In this time of such sorrow, we must face very important questions:

1. Was our loved one a child of the King? The Bible tells us in John 3:16, "For God so loved the world that He gave His only begotten Son, that whoever believes in Him should not perish but have everlasting life." So, anyone who asks Christ to come into their heart has *everlasting* life in heaven with the Father. First, an individual must recognize that it is possible to be religious without being a child of God. There are many people who go to church, give money to church, and do good deeds but have never made a commitment to Christ. They think their good works will get them into heaven; this simply isn't so.

Second, until an individual sees a need for help, God will not help them. Many people in our society think that they can do anything they want to without the help of God. In this life, it is true. But in the next life, they will find that judgment waits.

Third, as an individual realizes that God can give them hope, they turn to God. In turning to God, an individual needs to see that his life is without hope. Once we are in a hopeless condition, we start looking for answers.

Fourth, the individual realizes that the only hope for anyone is found in the Bible. Jesus often met with religious individuals during His lifetime here on this earth. In one particular instance, He talked with a man named Nicodemus. This man was a teacher of the Jewish religion. He came to Jesus by night. He asked questions. God is never mad if we ask honest questions of Him. Nicodemus wanted to know what it meant to be born again. He didn't think we could enter our mother's womb a second time. He was right. Jesus told him what it really means to be born again spiritually: ". . . whoever believes in (God's Son) should not perish but have eternal life" (John 3:15).

Each person must realize that he is outside of the kingdom of God and can get in only by belief in Christ Jesus. What is involved in this belief? In John 3:6 we read: "That which is born of the flesh is flesh, and that which is born of the Spirit is spirit." How can we know if we are born of the Spirit? Romans 10:9–10 tells us, "That if you confess with your mouth the Lord Jesus and believe in your heart that God has raised Him from the dead, you will be saved. For with the heart one believes unto righteousness, and with the mouth confession is made unto salvation."

If we want to be born of the Spirit we have to confess and believe. We need to confess that we are people who have broken the rules of God. We have to admit that we are outcasts in the sight of God. We have to admit that we can't save ourselves. We have to believe that Jesus died on the Cross for our sins and that He was raised from the dead to give us eternal life in heaven. If we confess and believe, we have eternal life. The King will accept us into His kingdom of heaven.

2. Was our loved one condemned by the King? Let's return to John chapter three again. In verse 18 we read: "He who believes in Him is not condemned; but he who does not believe is condemned already, because he has not believed in the name of the only begotten Son of God. Here we see that belief in Christ takes condemnation away from an individual. Only not believing condemns someone, *nothing else can*. John 3:36 tells us that there is a place God has prepared for those who do not believe in Him. Only those who commit this sin will be condemned.

3. Can anyone or anything take a believer out of the Father's hand? Now we have to ask ourselves about our loved one who has left this world. Is he/she someone who has accepted Christ as his/her personal Savior? There are only two who know the answer: our loved one and God. We have to leave our loved one in the hands of a holy and just God. Remember John 10:28–29: "And I give them eternal life, and they shall never perish; neither shall anyone snatch them out of My hand. My Father, who has given them to Me, is greater than all; and no one is able to snatch them out of My Father's hand." Once someone enters the family of God he will never leave, no matter what happens in this life.

Conclusion: In such a time of great sorrow and distress, we can trust God with our loved one. The question that remains with us is this: have we accepted Christ as our personal Savior, so we can join our loved ones in heaven? I would encourage you today to make a commitment to confess and believe in the Lord Jesus Christ. There is only one unpardonable sin that will keep us out of heaven: never confess and believe in the Lord Jesus Christ, who died on the Cross for our sins, who was buried in a tomb for three days and then on the third day rose from the dead. Don't make this mistake. Here in the midst of death, we are given an opportunity for eternal life!

Benediction: "Let not your heart be troubled; you believe in God, believe also in Me. In My Father's house are many mansions; if it were not so, I would have told you. I go to prepare a place for you. And if I go and prepare a place for you, I will come again and receive you to Myself; that where I am, there you may be also" (John 14:1–3).

Funeral Sermon:
For a Non-Christian
By Rev. Richard Sharpe

Choices

Today we have gathered in honor and memory of

_____

(Personal Comments)

Scripture: Luke 16:19–31

Introduction: This life is full of choices. We make over a hundred decisions each day. We have to decide what time to get up. We have to make a decision on what clothes to wear for the day or for work and then another set for home. We have to decide which way to go to work or to even go to work. We have to take care of other things all day long. The choices are always before us. We can never face a day without choices. Well, today we have a choice to make. The choice is where we are going to spend eternity. Some of us have made that choice. Others don't want to think about it. One day that choice will be final. As we gather in honor of our friend, we are faced with an important question; where will we spend eternity when we leave this earth?

1. **Two Men:** We read in the Gospel of Luke about two men. Some call this a parable, but parables don't usually use proper names. We are given a vivid account of two types of people.

   A. *The first man we read about is a rich man:* "There was a certain rich man who was clothed in purple and fine linen and fared sumptuously every day" (v. 19). Here we learn a few things about this man: he was rich, he wore fine clothes, and he lived in luxury every day. This is a man who had everything money could buy. He had taken hold of life and lived it to the hilt. He had no worries from a human perspective. Everyone would like to live this way. We often wish that we could do anything we wanted to do and go any place we wanted to go without worrying about the cost. Here was that person. He did it his way. He didn't need anyone. He was independently wealthy.

B. *The second man we read about was Lazarus:* "But there was a certain beggar named Lazarus, full of sores, who was laid at his gate, desiring to be fed with the crumbs which fell from the rich man's table. Moreover the dogs came and licked his sores" (v. 20, 21). We also learn a few things about the second man: He was a beggar, he had no place to live except on the street, he was sick and full of sores, he was satisfied with crumbs from the rich man's table, his only friends were dogs, and dogs were his only medical help. Here is a man that no one really wants to be. He had nothing. He was looked down on by all those around him. He was friendless. Christ told this story to let people know that there are two types of individuals in the world: those who depend on themselves and those who depend on others. This beggar did trust in God for help and comfort, as we learn from the outcome of his death.

2. **Two Choices:** Not only did these men differ in their lifestyle, they also differed greatly in their personal choices. All of us have the same choices to make.

A. *Lazarus:* "So it was that the beggar died, and was carried by the angels to Abraham's bosom" (v. 22). The beggar Lazarus died, but he had no known burial. He was carried by angels to this place of comfort, also referred to as Abraham's bosom; we learn later that this is a place called paradise by Christ (Luke 23:43). Paradise, or Abraham's bosom, is a place for those who believe in Jesus Christ to save them from the punishment of sin, and give their lives to Him as Lord; Lazarus made this choice.

B. *The Rich Man:*

"... the rich man also died and was buried. And in Hades he lifted up his eyes, being in torment, and saw Abraham far away, and Lazarus in his bosom. And he cried out and said, 'Father Abraham, have mercy on me, and send Lazarus, that he may dip the tip of his finger in water and cool off my tongue, for I am in agony in this flame.' But Abraham said, 'Child, remember that during your life you received your good things, and likewise Lazarus bad things; but now he is being comforted here, and you are in agony. And besides all this, between us and you there is a great chasm fixed, in order that those who wish to come over from here to you may not be able, and that none may cross over from there to us.' And he said, 'Then I beg you, Father, that you send him to my father's house—for I have five brothers—that he may warn them, lest they also come to this place of torment.' But Abraham said, 'They have Moses and the Prophets; let them hear them.' But he said, 'No, Father Abraham, but if someone goes to them from the dead, they will repent!' But he said to him, 'If they do not listen to Moses and the Prophets, neither will they

be persuaded if someone rises from the dead'"
(Luke 16:22–31, NASB).

So the rich man also dies. He has a funeral and is
buried. The rich man goes to a place called Hades or
hell, which is a place of torment. While he is there,
the rich man wants mercy; he quickly learns that after death there is no mercy. He also learned from
Abraham that the Bible is the only source of learning about life after death. Most of all he learned that
the choices made in life affect our eternal life. The
rich man made the wrong choice; he ignored Scripture, the book that directs us to Jesus and eternal
life!

Conclusion: Each one here today has a choice to make
concerning eternity. We can choose to believe in Christ,
following Him as Lord, or we can live for ourselves with no
hope for the future. If we choose Jesus Christ, then there
needs to be a change that includes confession of sin and belief in the gospel of Christ. This gospel tells us that Christ
died on the Cross for our sins, He was buried, and He rose
from the dead to show us the way to heaven. If you want
more information regarding this way of life, please see me
after the service.

The second choice is to go our own way and live as if
this life was the only place that matters. Once this choice is
made, we will have to live with this decision for all eternity.
Remember, that being rich doesn't mean you cannot go to
heaven. There are some rich people who know Christ. But
if we trust in our riches or anything else more than Christ,
we may find ourselves in a place of torment for eternity.

Our friend, in whose honor we gather this day, has already made his/her choice. God is just and merciful, and

only He knows the decisions made by our friend. The question to consider, as we are faced with the reality of life and death, is what choice will you make?

Benediction: "Now to Him who is able to keep you from stumbling, and to make you stand in the presence of His glory blameless with great joy, to the only God our Savior, through Jesus Christ our Lord, be glory, majesty, dominion and authority, before all time and now and forever. Amen" (Jude 24–25, NASB).

Graveside/Committal Services
By Rev. Mark Hollis

Along with the funeral sermon, the graveside service should be adapted for the burial of a Christian or a non-Christian. Sometimes the graveside service replaces the funeral; other times it follows the funeral. Each of these variations has been outlined.

The Graveside/Committal Service
Following the Funeral for a Believer

Sample Order of Service

Scripture Reading

Committal

Prayer for Comfort

Benediction

Sample Detailed Service

The minister stands in front or beside the casket and addresses the family. These are the final words before the burial and should be filled with hope.

Scripture Reading: "Now I saw a new heaven and a new earth, for the first heaven and the first earth had passed away. Also there was no more sea. Then I, John, saw the holy city, New Jerusalem, coming down out of heaven from God, prepared as a bride adorned for her husband. And I heard a loud voice from heaven saying, "Behold, the tabernacle of God is with men, and He will dwell with them, and they shall be His people. God Himself will be with them and be their God. And God will wipe away every tear from their eyes; there shall be no more death, nor sorrow, nor crying. There shall be no more pain, for the former things have passed away." Then He who sat on the throne said, "Behold, I make all things new." And He said to me, "Write, for these words are true and faithful." And He said to me, "It is done! I am the Alpha and the Omega, the Beginning and the End. I will give of the fountain of the water of life freely to him who thirsts. He who overcomes shall inherit all things, and I will be his God and he shall be My son (Revelation 21:1–7).

We have gathered here to commit to rest the body of our loved one and friend:

"The LORD is my light and my salvation; whom shall I fear? The LORD is the strength of my life; Of whom shall I be afraid? One thing I have desired of the Lord, that will I seek: that I may dwell in the house of the Lord all the days of my life, to behold the beauty of the Lord, and to inquire in His temple" (Psalm 27:1, 4).

Committal: Some of us have shared through these passing years a wonderful companionship and fellowship with our faithful brother (or sister). We cherish the many blessed and hallowed memories that come to us in these moments. His (Her) faithfulness, friendship, and consecrated life will continue their radiance and testimony in our lives. In the name of Jesus Christ whom he (she) loved and served, we commit his (her) body to rest, knowing that his (her) spirit is with the Lord in His heavenly house. In so doing, we rest our hearts in fresh confidence upon the sure and certain hope of the resurrection to life through Jesus Christ, "Who will transform our lowly body that it may be conformed to His glorious body, according to the working by which He is able even to subdue all things to Himself (Philippians 3:21).

Prayer for Comfort: *The minister may use his own words or the following prayer:*

Father, we gather in this solemn place to remember the life and mourn the death of our loved one. We do not sorrow as those who have no hope, for our hope is in Jesus Christ. We ask that You would comfort each family member and friend. May they be comforted by Your Word, encouraged through happy memories, and sustained by the hope of the resurrection for all who place their faith in You. Amen.

Benediction: "The LORD bless you and keep you; the LORD make His face shine upon you, and be gracious to you; the LORD lift up His countenance upon you, and give you peace (Numbers 6:24–26).

Following the benediction the minister shakes the hand of immediate family members.

The Graveside/Committal Service
Following the Funeral for the Non-Christian

Sample Order of Service

Scripture Reading   *Prayer for Comfort*

Committal   *Benediction*

Sample Detailed Service

The minister stands in front or beside the casket and addresses the family. These are the final words before the burial and should be filled with hope.

Scripture Reading: "To everything there is a season, a time for every purpose under heaven: a time to be born, and a time to die; a time to plant, and a time to pluck what is planted; a time to kill, and a time to heal; a time to break down, and a time to build up; a time to weep, and a time to laugh; a time to mourn, and a time to dance; a time to cast away stones, and a time to gather stones; a time to embrace, and a time to refrain from embracing; a time to gain, and a time to lose; a time to keep, and a time to throw away; a time to tear, and a time to sew; a time to keep silence, and a time to speak; a time to love, and a time to hate; a time of war, and a time of peace" (Ecclesiastes 3:1–8).

Committal: We have gathered here to commit to rest the body of our loved one and friend. Here is the form of one whose memory we shall treasure. Some of us have shared through these passing years a wonderful companionship with our loved one. Let us cherish the many memories that come to us at this time and let each of us here purpose to seek the Lord with all our hearts and respond to the opportunities of salvation extended to us through His grace.

"The LORD is my light and my salvation; whom shall I fear? The LORD is the strength of my life; of whom shall I be afraid?" (Psalm 27:1).

"We then, as workers together with Him also plead with you not to receive the grace of God in vain. For He says: 'In an acceptable time I have heard you, and in the day of salvation I have helped you.' Behold, now is the accepted time; behold, now is the day of salvation" (2 Corinthians 6:1–2).

"Seek the LORD while He may be found, call upon Him while He is near" (Isaiah 55:6).

Earth to earth, ashes to ashes, dust to dust. "Shall not the Judge of all the earth do right?" (Genesis 18:25).

Prayer for Comfort: Father, we gather in this solemn place to remember the life and mourn the death of our loved one. We ask that You would comfort each family member and friend. May they turn to Your Word for comfort, be encouraged through happy memories, and purpose in their heart to seek You while You may be found. Amen.

Benediction: "The LORD bless you and keep you; the LORD make His face shine upon you, and be gracious to you; the LORD lift up His countenance upon you, and give you peace" (Numbers 6:24 26).

Following the benediction the minister shakes the hand of immediate family members.

Graveside/Committal Service
in Place of the Funeral for the Believer

Sample Order of Service

Opening Scripture   *Committal*

Remembering   *Prayer for Comfort*

Scripture Reading   *Benediction*

Sample Detailed Service

Some families will request a graveside service instead of a service in the chapel or church. While this service may be longer than the typical committal, keep in mind weather circumstances which might necessitate keeping it as short as possible.

The minister stands in front or beside the casket and addresses the family. These are the final words before the burial and should be filled with hope.

Opening Scripture: We gather here today to celebrate the life and mourn the death of our loved one.

"The eternal God is your refuge, and underneath are the everlasting arms; He will thrust out the enemy from before you, and will say, 'Destroy!'" (Deuteronomy 33:27).

"The LORD is my shepherd; I shall not want. He makes me to lie down in green pastures; He leads me beside the still waters. He restores my soul; He leads me in the paths of righteousness for His name s sake. Yea, though I walk through the valley of the shadow of death, I will fear no evil; for You are with me; Your rod and Your staff, they comfort me. You prepare a table before me in the presence of my enemies; You anoint my head with oil; my cup runs over. Surely goodness and mercy shall follow me all the days of my life; and I will dwell in the house of the Lord forever" (Psalm 23:1–6).

"God is our refuge and strength, a very present help in trouble" (Psalm 46:1).

Remembering: Choose one or two of the following: read the obituary, share a memory regarding the deceased (personal or one shared with you by a family member), have a friend or family member of the deceased share a memory, ask those assembled to think of their favorite memory of the deceased (What made him laugh? Was there a story she loved to share? Was there a song he loved to sing?)

At times like these we are comforted by the memories of the one we loved. Though we are sad, we do not grieve as those who have no hope. We know that to be absent from the body is to be present with the Lord.

Scripture Reading: "For if we believe that Jesus died and rose again, even so God will bring with Him those who have fallen asleep in Jesus. For this we say to you by the word of the Lord, that we who are alive and remain until the coming of the Lord will by no means precede those who are asleep. For the Lord Himself will descend from heaven with a shout, with the voice of the archangel, and with the trumpet of God. And the dead in Christ will rise first. Then we who are alive and remain shall be caught up together with them in the clouds to meet the Lord in the air. And thus we shall always be with the Lord" (1 Thessalonians 4:14–17).

Committal: Some of us have shared through these passing years a wonderful companionship and fellowship with our faithful brother (or sister). We cherish the many blessed and hallowed memories that come to us in these moments. His (Her) faithfulness, friendship and consecrated life will continue their radiance and testimony in our lives. In the name of Jesus Christ whom he (she) loved and served, we commit his (her) body to rest, knowing that his (her) spirit is with the Lord in His heavenly house. In so doing, we rest our hearts in fresh confidence upon the sure and certain hope of the resurrection to life through Jesus Christ, "Who will transform our lowly body that it may be conformed to His glorious body, according to the working by which He is able even to subdue all things to Himself" (Philippians 3:21).

Prayer for Comfort: *The minister may use his own words or the following prayer:*

Father, we gather in this solemn place to remember the life and mourn the death of our loved one. We do not sorrow as those who have no hope, for our hope is in Jesus Christ. We ask that You would comfort each family member and friend. May they be comforted by Your Word, encouraged through happy memories, and sustained by the hope of the resurrection for all who place their faith in You. Amen.

Benediction: "The Lord bless you and keep you; the Lord make His face shine upon you, and be gracious to you; the Lord lift up His countenance upon you, and give you peace" (Numbers 6:24–26).

Following the benediction the minister shakes the hand of immediate family members.

Graveside/Committal Service
in Place of the Funeral for the Non-Christian

Sample Order of Service

Opening Scripture   *Committal*

Remembering   *Prayer for Comfort*

Scripture Reading   *Benediction*

Sample Detailed Service

The minister stands in front or beside the casket and addresses the family. These are the final words before the burial and should be filled with hope.

Opening Scripture: "The Lord is my shepherd; I shall not want. He makes me to lie down in green pastures; He leads me beside the still waters. He restores my soul; He leads me in the paths of righteousness for His name's sake. Yea, though I walk through the valley of the shadow of death, I will fear no evil; for You are with me; Your rod and Your staff, they comfort me. You prepare a table before me in the presence of my enemies; You anoint my head with oil; my cup runs over. Surely goodness and mercy shall follow me all the days of my life; and I will dwell in the house of the Lord forever" (Psalm 23:1–6).

Remembering: *Choose one or two of the following: read the obituary, share a memory regarding the deceased (personal or one shared with you by a family member), have a friend or family member of the deceased share a memory, ask those assembled to think of their favorite* *memory of the deceased (What made him laugh? Was there a story she loved to share? Was there a song he loved to sing?)*

Scripture Reading: "To everything there is a season, a time for every purpose under heaven: a time to be born, and a time to die; a time to plant, and a time to pluck what is planted; a time to kill, and a time to heal; a time to break down, and a time to build up; a time to weep, and a time to laugh; a time to mourn, and a time to dance; a time to cast away stones, and a time to gather stones; a time to embrace, and a time to refrain from embracing; a time to gain, and a time to lose; a time to keep, and a time to throw away; a time to tear, and a time to sew; a time to keep silence, and a time to speak; a time to love, and a time to hate; a time of war, and a time of peace" (Ecclesiastes 3:1–8).

Committal: We have gathered here to commit to rest the body of our loved one and friend. Here is the form of one whose memory we shall treasure. Some of us have shared through these passing years a wonderful companionship with our loved one. Let us cherish the many memories that come to us at this time and let each of us here purpose to seek the Lord with all our hearts and respond to the opportunities of salvation extended to us through His grace.

"The LORD is my light and my salvation; whom shall I fear? The LORD is the strength of my life; of whom shall I be afraid?" (Psalm 27:1).

"We then, as workers together with Him also plead with you not to receive the grace of God in vain. For He says: 'In an acceptable time I have heard you, and in the day of salvation I have helped you.' Behold, now is the accepted time; behold, now is the day of salvation" (2 Corinthians 6:1–2).

"Seek the Lord while He may be found, call upon Him while He is near" (Isaiah 55:6).

Earth to earth, ashes to ashes, dust to dust. "Shall not the Judge of all the earth do right?" (Genesis 18:25).

Prayer for Comfort: *The minister may use his own words or the following prayer:*

Father, we gather in this solemn place to remember the life and mourn the death of our loved one. We ask that You would comfort each family member and friend. May they turn to Your Word for comfort, be encouraged through happy memories, and purpose in their heart to seek You while You may be found. Amen.

Benediction: "The Lord bless you and keep you; the Lord make His face shine upon you, and be gracious to you; the Lord lift up His countenance upon you, and give you peace" (Numbers 6:24 26).

Following the benediction the minister shakes the hand of immediate family members.

Memorial Service

The funeral service is often a time of sorrow and grieving. While this is also true at the memorial service, it should also include inspiration, laughter, and a time to re-focus. The memorial service should encourage the audience to honor the memory of their loved one by reflecting on their own goals, accomplishments, and character and making necessary changes.

A Sample Order of Service for a Memorial Service

Prelude

Hymn

Scripture Reading

Special Music

Invocation

Introductory Remarks

A Time of Remembrance

Concluding Remarks

Prayer

Benediction

A Sample Detailed Memorial Service

Prelude: *The organist or pianist should play appropriate music. Hymns which could be played are* Safe in the Arms of Jesus, The Old Rugged Cross, Beyond the Sunset, Amazing Grace, It Is Well With My Soul, *and* Abide with Me. *The minister should check with the family and see if the deceased had any favorite hymns that could be used at this point.*

Hymn: *Sung by choir, soloist, congregation, or selected group.*

Scripture Reading: Have you not known? Have you not heard? The everlasting God, the Lord, the Creator of the ends of the earth, neither faints nor is weary. His understanding is unsearchable. He gives power to the weak, and to those who have no might He increases strength. But those who wait on the Lord shall renew their strength; they shall mount up with wings like eagles, they shall run and not be weary, they shall walk and not faint (Isaiah 40:28–29, 31).

For I am persuaded that neither death nor life, nor angels nor principalities nor powers, nor things present nor things to come, nor height nor depth, nor any other created thing, shall be able to separate us from the love of God which is in Christ Jesus our Lord (Romans 8:38–39).

Special Music: Sung by choir, selected group, or soloist. This music could be selected by the family.

Invocation: Father, may your Spirit guide us as we reflect on Your work in the life of our departed loved one, and in our own. In Jesus' name, Amen.

Introductory Remarks: We gather today in memory of
_____ not only to honor him/her in
death, but to remember his/her life. Our loved one would not
want us only to be sad and grieved, but to remember his/
her life. Let us take a moment to reflect on his/her life.

The pastor should then call the first friend/family mem-
ber to the front. The well-equipped minister might carry
a pocket pack of tissues to help the speaker avoid em-
barrassment should he/she be overwhelmed in tears.

A Time of Remembrance: *Each family member, friend,*
or associate of the deceased shall now present his/her
own memories.

Concluding Remarks: *If the pastor has been a close per-*
sonal friend of the deceased, he should now add, briefly,
his own memories and comments. If not, he may con-
clude:

When we pause to remember the life of _____,
we are forced to reflect on our own lives. What are our
goals? What is really worthwhile and important?

Jesus, in the midst of a crowd of followers, turned to
one man and said, "Follow me." But the man said, "Lord,
let me first go and bury my father." Jesus told him, "Let the
dead bury their own dead, but you go and preach the kingdom of God" (from Luke 9:59–60).

Jesus is not telling us to neglect the burial of our loved
ones, but He is teaching us what is more important, to
preach the kingdom of God! Jesus Himself wept at Lazarus's grave, but it motivated Him to action! We should not
focus too long on death, but we should allow it to inspire

us to preach life, life found only through Jesus Christ who said, "I am the way, the truth, and the life. No one comes to the Father except through Me" (John 14:6).

Prayer: Lord, help us to know what is most important in this life and to live for you alone. Comfort our grieving hearts, and bless the memories of our dear loved one. In Jesus' name, Amen.

Benediction: "Fear not, for I am with you; be not dismayed, for I am your God. I will strengthen you, yes, I will help you, I will uphold you with My righteous right hand" (Isaiah 41:10).

Traditional Funeral Scriptures

Deuteronomy 33:27: The eternal God is your refuge, and underneath are the everlasting arms.

Job 19:25–26: For I know that my Redeemer lives . . . and after my skin is destroyed, this I know, that in my flesh I shall see God.

Psalm 23:1–6: The LORD is my shepherd; I shall not want. He makes me to lie down in green pastures; He leads me beside the still waters. He restores my soul; He leads me in the paths of righteousness for His name's sake. Yea, though I walk through the valley of the shadow of death, I will fear no evil; for You are with me; Your rod and Your staff, they comfort me. You prepare a table before me in the presence of my enemies; You anoint my head with oil; my cup runs over. Surely goodness and mercy shall follow me all the days of my life; and I will dwell in the house of the LORD forever.

Psalm 27:1: The LORD is my light and my salvation; whom shall I fear? The LORD is the strength of my life; of whom shall I be afraid?

Psalm 42:11: Why are you cast down, O my soul? And why are you disquieted within me? Hope in God; for I shall yet praise Him, the help of my countenance and my God.

Psalm 46:1–2: God is our refuge and strength, a very present help in trouble. Therefore we will not fear, even though the earth be removed, and though the mountains be carried into the midst of the sea.

Psalm 91:1: He who dwells in the secret place of the Most High shall abide under the shadow of the Almighty.

Isaiah 40:28–29, 31: Have you not known? Have you not heard? The everlasting God, the LORD, the Creator of the ends of the earth, neither faints nor is weary. His understanding is unsearchable. He gives power to the weak, and to those who have no might He increases strength. . . . But those who wait on the Lord shall renew their strength; they shall mount up with wings like eagles, they shall run and not be weary, they shall walk and not faint.

Isaiah 41:10: Fear not, for I am with you; be not dismayed, for I am your God. I will strengthen you, yes, I will help you, I will uphold you with My righteous right hand.

Isaiah 43:1–3: "Fear not, for I have redeemed you; I have called you by your name; you are Mine. When you pass through the waters, I will be with you; and through the rivers, they shall not overflow you. When you walk through the fire, you shall not be burned, nor shall the flame scorch you. For I am the Lord your God, the Holy One of Israel, your Savior."

Nahum 1:7: The LORD is good, a stronghold in the day of trouble; and He knows those who trust in Him.

Matthew 5:4: "Blessed are those who mourn, for they shall be comforted."

Matthew 28:20: ". . . and lo, I am with you always, even to the end of the age."

John 11:25: Jesus said to her, "I am the resurrection and the life. He who believes in Me, though he may die, he shall live."

John 14:1–6: "Let not your heart be troubled; you believe in God, believe also in Me. In My Father's house are many mansions; if it were not so, I would have told you. I go to prepare a place for you. And if I go and prepare a place for you, I will come again and receive you to Myself; that where I am, there you may be also. And where I go you know, and the way you know." Thomas said to Him, "Lord, we do not know where You are going, and how can we know the way?" Jesus said to him, "I am the way, the truth, and the life. No one comes to the Father except through Me."

John 14:27: "Peace I leave with you, My peace I give to you; not as the world gives do I give to you. Let not your heart be troubled, neither let it be afraid."

John 16:33: "These things I have spoken to you, that in Me you may have peace. In the world you will have tribulation; but be of good cheer, I have overcome the world."

Romans 8:38–39: For I am persuaded that neither death nor life, nor angels nor principalities nor powers, nor things present nor things to come, nor height nor depth, nor any other created thing, shall be able to separate us from the love of God which is in Christ Jesus our Lord.

1 Corinthians 15:51–57: Behold, I tell you a mystery: we shall not all sleep, but we shall all be changed in a moment, in the twinkling of an eye, at the last trumpet. For the trumpet will sound, and the dead will be raised incorruptible, and we shall be changed. For this corruptible must put on incorruption, and this mortal must put on immortality.

So when this corruptible has put on incorruption, and this mortal has put on immortality, then shall be brought to pass the saying that is written: "Death is swallowed up in victory." "O Death, where is your sting? O Hades, where is your victory?" The sting of death is sin, and the strength of sin is the law. But thanks be to God, who gives us the victory through our Lord Jesus Christ.

2 Corinthians 1:3–4: Blessed be the God and Father of our Lord Jesus Christ, the Father of mercies and God of all comfort, who comforts us in all our tribulation.

2 Corinthians 5:1, 6, 8: For we know that if our earthly house, this tent, is destroyed, we have a building from God, a house not made with hands, eternal in the heavens. So we are always confident, knowing that while we are at home in the body we are absent from the Lord. We are confident, yes, well pleased rather to be absent from the body and to be present with the Lord.

2 Corinthians 12:9: "My grace is sufficient for you, for My strength is made perfect in weakness."

Philippians 1:21–23: For to me, to live is Christ, and to die is gain. But if I live on in the flesh, this will mean fruit from my labor; yet what I shall choose I cannot tell. For I am hard-pressed between the two, having a desire to depart and be with Christ, which is far better.

Philippians 3:20–21: For our citizenship is in heaven, from which we also eagerly wait for the Savior, the Lord Jesus Christ, who will transform our lowly body that it may be conformed to His glorious body, according to the working by which He is able even to subdue all things to Himself.

1 Thessalonians 4:13–18, NASB: But we do not want you to be uninformed, brethren, about those who are asleep, that you may not grieve, as do the rest who have no hope. For if we believe that Jesus died and rose again, even so God will bring with Him those who have fallen asleep in Jesus. For this we say to you by the word of the Lord, that we who are alive, and remain until the coming of the Lord, shall not precede those who have fallen asleep. For the Lord Himself will descend from heaven with a shout, with the voice of the archangel and with the trumpet of God, and the dead in Christ will rise first. Then we who are alive and remain will be caught up together with them in the clouds to meet the Lord in the air, and thus we shall always be with the Lord. Therefore comfort one another with these words.

2 Timothy 4:7–8: I have fought the good fight, I have finished the race, I have kept the faith. Finally, there is laid up for me the crown of righteousness, which the Lord, the righteous Judge, will give to me on that Day, and not to me only but also to all who have loved His appearing.

Hebrews 13:5: For He Himself has said, "I will never leave you nor forsake you."

1 Peter 1:3–9: Blessed be the God and Father of our Lord Jesus Christ, who according to His abundant mercy has begotten us again to a living hope through the resurrection of Jesus Christ from the dead, to an inheritance incorruptible and undefiled and that does not fade away, reserved in heaven for you, who are kept by the power of God through faith for salvation ready to be revealed in the last time. In this you greatly rejoice, though now for a little while, if need be, you have been grieved by various trials, that the genuineness of your faith, being much more precious than gold that perishes, though it is tested by fire, may be found to praise, honor, and glory at the revelation of Jesus Christ, whom having not seen you love. Though now you do not see Him, yet believing, you rejoice with joy inexpressible and full of glory, receiving the end of your faith—the salvation of your souls.

1 John 3:2: Beloved, now we are children of God; and it has not yet been revealed what we shall be, but we know that when He is revealed, we shall be like Him, for we shall see Him as He is.

Revelation 7:13–17: Then one of the elders answered, saying to me, "Who are these arrayed in white robes, and where did they come from?" And I said to him, "Sir, you know." So he said to me, "These are the ones who come out of the great tribulation, and washed their robes and made them white in the blood of the Lamb. Therefore they are before the throne of God, and serve Him day and night in His temple. And He who sits on the throne will dwell among them. They shall neither hunger anymore nor thirst anymore; the sun shall not strike them, nor any heat; for the Lamb who is in the midst of the throne will shepherd them and lead them to living fountains of waters. And God will wipe away every tear from their eyes."

Revelation 14:13: Then I heard a voice from heaven saying to me, "Write: 'Blessed are the dead who die in the Lord from now on.'" "Yes," says the Spirit, "that they may rest from their labors, and their works follow them."

Traditional Funeral Hymns
by Jerry Carraway

Asleep in Jesus, Margaret MacKay/William B. Bladbury; Public Domain.

I'll Have a New Life, Luther G. Presley; © 1940. Renewed 1968 Stamps-Baxter Music (Admin. by Brentwood-Benson Music.)

I'll Meet You In the Morning, Albert E. Brumley; © 1936 Hartford Music Company. 1964 Albert E. Brumley and Sons (Admin. by Integrated Copyright Group, Inc.)

Just a Little While, Eugene M. Bartlett, © E. M. Bartlett. Renewed 1949 Albert E. Brumley and Sons (Admin. by Integrated Copyright Group, Inc.)

When I've Traveled My Last Mile, Henry J. Donohue; © 1941. (Renewed 1969 Stamps-Baxter Music, Inc.)

Abide With Me, Henry F. Lyte/William H. Monk; Public Domain.

Be Still My Soul, Katharina Von Schlegal/Jane L. Borthwick/Jean Sibelius; Public Domain.

Near to the Heart of God, Cleland McAfee; Public Domain.

O God, Our Help In Ages Past, Isaac Watts/William Croft; Public Domain.

Precious Lord, Take My Hand, Thomas A. Dorsey; © 1938. (Renewed) by Warner-Tamberlane Publishing Corporation.

Sweet Beulah Land, Squire Parsons, Jr.; © 1979 Kingsmen Publishing Company (Admin. by Brentwood-Benson Music Publishing, Inc.)

Dedications

Child/Infant Dedication
By Rev. Richard Sharpe

The dedication of an infant rarely is the central feature of a worship service. Most often, it occurs at the end of the service. In a worship service in which a child or infant will be dedicated, some ministers may wish to preach on the subject of children, parenting, or the church's involvement in either of these. The following is a sample outline that might be used, followed by an order of service for the child or infant dedication.

Awesome Gift

Scripture: Deuteronomy 6:4–9

Hear, O Israel: the LORD our God, the Lord is one! You shall love the LORD your God with all your heart, with all your soul, and with all your strength. And these words which I command you today shall be in your heart. You shall teach them diligently to your children, and shall talk of them when you sit in your house, when you walk by the way, when you lie down, and when you rise up. You shall bind them as a sign on your hand, and they shall be as frontlets between your eyes. You shall write them on the doorposts of your house and on your gates.

Introduction: I presently have five grandchildren. I have watched three of them be dedicated to the Lord. All of my children were dedicated to the Lord as babies. All of my children have accepted Christ as their personal Savior. All of my children have married Christian spouses. This is not always the case with every child dedicated to the Lord, but the importance of parents starting their children out right cannot be measured by any earthly standard. God wants us to realize that our children are a gift from Him. They are an awesome gift. What are we going to do with our gifts from Him?

1. Our responsibility is to be faithful to our Lord. The first responsibility of parents is to love the Lord with all their heart, soul, and might. What does this mean? It means that before a parent can dedicate their children to the Lord, they must love the Lord themselves. There are many parents who go through the motions with their Christianity. They do what is expected of them by the rest of their church. They bring their children to be dedicated because it is a tradition. The problem is that it is a biblical tradition and the Bible has some rules regarding dedicating children to Him. The first rule is that parents must be right with God. They must be ones who are faithfully studying the Word, praying, fasting, worshiping, serving, and practicing the disciplines of the faith. They must do it because God is worthy of their love and worship. Their eyes must be focused on the Lord.

2. Our responsibility is to be examples for our Lord. Secondly, parents need to be examples to their children. They have to be the ones who sing praises to the Lord—not just in church but at home. They must be the ones who read the Bible for themselves and then have family devotions with the children. They have to be the ones who attend church regularly with a cheerful attitude. They are to be the ones who give their money to the church with a smile on their face. Some parents are good examples of what it means to be a Christian on Sunday, but those who dedicate their children should be ones who serve God the rest of the week as well. I have met many parents who say that they don't want to force their children to go to church because they were forced to go to church. They want their children to make the choice when they grow up and can choose for themselves. This presents a problem; eighteen years may pass in which the child never sets foot in the church. What, then, would be the obvious choice? Going to church or sleeping in? Usually it's the latter. We have our children eat, sleep, and do other things that we tell them to do. Their eternity is dependant on the example we set for them when they are children. If they are without any example of God in their youth, they will usually not make the right choice in adulthood.

3. Our responsibility is to be trainers of our children for the Lord. Our passage tells us that we need to train our children at all times in our lives:

    A. Train them when we are sitting down.
    B. Train them when we are walking
    C. Train them when we are lying down
    D. Train them with the Word of God in their hands
    E. Train them with the Word of God before their eyes on a regular basis
    F. Train them with the Word of God written on items in our home

Do you think this passage leaves any time out for us to train our children? There are many tools available to train our children. We need a plan from birth till they move out to train them for the Lord. Without a plan, they will never be trained and the enemy will work in their lives.

4. Our responsibility is to keep the Lord before our children always. There is not a day that should go by that we are not helping our children to understand the Lord better. There should not be a day that goes by that we are not learning new things from the Lord. We need to take up our cross daily and follow the Lord. Our first responsibility is to our spouse and our children. They are our first mission field. If we lose our family, we will have sorrow. Save yourselves the sorrow and do all you can to be the example you should be and train your children. The final results are in the Lord's hands, but we should do everything possible to point them to the Lord.

Conclusion: Some questions to consider:

1. Do you love the Lord with all your heart, soul, and might?
2. Do you want to train your children to love the Lord?
3. Do you have a plan to train them?
4. Do you set a good example for your children to follow?
5. Do you know the doctrines of the Bible?
6. Do you know the disciplines of the faith?
7. Do you know the books of the Bible?
8. Do you have a regular time of devotions for yourselves?
9. Do you have a regular time of devotions as a couple?
10. Do you have a regular time of devotions with your family?
11. Will this church help these parents to be the best examples they can be?
12. Will this church pray for these parents and their child/children from this day forward?
13. Will this church pray for the salvation of this child at an early age?

14. Will this church pray for this child to marry a saved spouse?
15. Will this church help with the training of this child?

Sample Child/Infant Dedication Service Outline

At the conclusion of the service the minister might have an invitation for parents who wish to dedicate themselves to Scriptural parenting, for children who might have gone astray, or for any general need. After the invitation, the minister should call the parents forward with their children.

Acknowledgment of the Parents or Guardians and Child

Dedicational Vows

Scripture Reading

Prayer of Dedication

Hymn or Benediction

Certificate of Dedication

Sample Detailed Child/Infant Dedication Service

Acknowledgment of the Parents or Guardians and Child: *The minister should be sure to note whether the parents or grandparents or other guardians are dedicating the child. He should also note whether or not additional family has come to witness the dedication.*

Brothers and sisters, today Mrs. *first name* and Mr. *first and last name* have come acknowledging and professing their dependence on the Lord to raise their child *child's full name*.

If the family so wishes, the minister may at this point ask the extended family to stand to acknowledge their part in the dedication.

Dedicational Vows

Minister: Parents (or guardians), do you come professing Jesus Christ as the Lord and Savior of your lives?

Parents: We do.

Minister: And do you come to dedicate yourselves to biblical instruction, discipline, and love of this child?

Parents: We do.

Minister: And do you come to dedicate *child's name* into the ultimate control and will of God through the Lord Jesus Christ?

Parents: We do.

Minister, turning to face the church: Do you, church, agree to support these parents (guardians) by your example and through acts of service; and do you agree to reinforce the biblical instruction, discipline, and love of this child under the supreme rule of the Lord Jesus Christ? If so, you may signify by standing.

The church members shall stand at this point.

Minister: You may be seated.

Scripture Reading: Hear, O Israel: the LORD our God, the LORD is one! You shall love the LORD your God with all your heart, with all your soul, and with all your strength. And these words which I command you today shall be in your heart. You shall teach them diligently to your children, and shall talk of them when you sit in your house, when you walk by the way, when you lie down, and when you rise up. You shall bind them as a sign on your hand, and they shall be as frontlets between your eyes. You shall write them on the doorposts of your house and on your gates (Deuteronomy 6:4–9).

Train up a child in the way he should go, and when he is old he will not depart from it (Proverbs 22:6).

Prayer of Dedication: *Some ministers may wish to, at this point, take the infant into his arms. Or, if the child is older, he may bend down and lay his hand upon the child's head or take the child's hand. Otherwise, the family might kneel together at the altar for the prayer of dedication.*

Father, we bring this child to You with all our heart, soul, and might. We want to raise this child to love You and serve You. Please help us to be the congregation and parents that will set the right example for this child, and that this child might love and serve You throughout his/her life. We pray this in Jesus' name. Amen.

Closing Hymn or Benediction

Certificate of Dedication: *The minister may give the parents a certificate of dedication immediately after the prayer of dedication. If so, at this point he might allow a picture to be made of the child with his/her parents for the bulletin and for the parents.*

Confirmation Service

Confirmation services vary greatly among denominations. In the Presbyterian Church, baptism and church membership confirmation are approved by the representatives of the congregation and the elected ruling elders who are ordained laypersons. In the Methodist Church, baptism and church membership confirmation are sanctioned by the local pastor or minister of a church. In the Episcopal Church, the local rector or priest may baptize individuals but confirmation and membership may only be facilitated by the Bishop. If the candidate for confirmation has not been baptized, he/she may be baptized and then confirmed in the same service. The following is a general sample service which may be adapted to fit any given congregation.

Sample Confirmation Order of Service

Presentation of Candidate for Confirmation

Address to the Candidate for Confirmation

Prayer of Dedication

Address to the Confirmed Church Member

Benediction, Hymn, or Prayer

Sample Detailed Confirmation Service

Presentation of Candidate for Confirmation: *At the end of a worship service, an elder or the minister should call the candidate for confirmation to stand and come to the front and shall say:*

Dearly beloved, we shall now receive _____ to the confirmation of his/her baptism. He/she has been received into the communicant membership of the church; he/she has received instruction in the church, and now he/she is ready to declare his/her faith publicly, and to be joined with us in the ministry of Jesus Christ.

Address to the Candidate for Confirmation: *The minister shall turn to the candidate for confirmation and say:*

Child of God, in your baptism you were sealed and given a sign of your union with Jesus Christ. God in all His holiness and goodness has kept you and guarded you. Now you have come to an age in which you recognize these things, understanding fully the gospel of Jesus Christ. Now you desire to come before God and the church to acknowledge these things. You wish to publicly profess your faith in the Lord Jesus Christ, giving yourself fully to Him and His service, just as He said, "Therefore whoever confesses Me before men, him I will also confess before My Father who is in heaven" (Matthew 10:32).

The minister shall ask a series of questions to the candidate:

In some traditions, the Apostles' Creed is read to the candidate to affirm these beliefs.

Minister: Do you believe in God, the Father Almighty, Creator of heaven and earth, and in Jesus Christ, His only Son, our Lord?

Candidate: I do.

Minister: Do you promise to be a faithful disciple of Jesus Christ, through the power of the Holy Spirit, displaying His love and obeying His Word?

Candidate: I do.

Minister: Do you now confirm the vows which were taken for you in your baptism?

Candidate: I do.

Minister: Do you, in humility and faith, place all your trust in the hands of our merciful God through Jesus Christ?

Candidate: I do.

Minister: Do you give yourself to being a steward of the grace given to you, sharing faithfully in the worship and service of Jesus Christ and His church? And will you give generously as the Lord prospers you? And will you give your whole self to the worship and service of Jesus Christ and His kingdom throughout the earth?

Candidate: I do.

Prayer of Dedication: In the presence of these witnesses, you have publicly confirmed your faith; so now let us join together in prayer before the Lord.

Almighty God, we ask that You strengthen Your servant. Bless him/her abundantly with Your Holy Spirit. Increase his/her understanding of You, his/her zeal for You, and his/her love for You. Keep him/her in Your mercy and grace throughout eternity. We pray in Jesus' name, Amen.

Often, there are several candidates for confirmation: if so, the minister may lay his hands on the heads of each one, praying:

Lord, guard Your servant in Your grace that he/she might grow in knowledge, obedience, zeal, and love in Your Holy Spirit day by day until the day of our Lord Jesus Christ. Amen.

Address to the Confirmed Church Member: *The minister shall ask for the congregation to stand and shall say:*

Now, having confessed your faith, I, in the name of the Lord Jesus Christ, admit you into the fellowship of the church as a confirmed member, "Therefore, whether you eat or drink, or whatever you do, do all to the glory of God" (1 Corinthians 10:31).

Now I commission you as Christ commissioned His disciples, "Go therefore and make disciples of all the nations, baptizing them in the name of the Father and of the Son and of the Holy Spirit, teaching them to observe all things that I have commanded you; and lo, I am with you always, even to the end of the age." Amen (Matthew 28:19–20).

Benediction, Hymn, or Prayer: *The minister may use the above passage as his concluding benediction, or may choose another passage for the benediction, or may close in an appropriate hymn or in prayer.*

Building Dedication
By Dr. Melvin Worthington

A Sample Order of Service for Building Dedication

Prelude

Welcome/Greetings

Hymn

Prayer

Special Music

Hymn

Special Recognitions

Greetings from the Community

Greetings from the Denomination

History of the Church

Special Music

Sermon

Act of Dedication

Prayer of Dedication

Benediction

Postlude

A Sample Detailed Order of Service
for Building Dedication

Prelude: *Musicians should play appropriate selections of hymns relating to the occasion. Selections could include:* A Mighty Fortress, Great Is Thy Faithfulness, Guide Me O Thou Great Jehovah, O Our God in Ages Past, *and* How Great Thou Art.

Welcome/Greetings: *The church family and friends should be greeted and welcomed at this point.*

Hymn: *Hymn selection could include:* All the Way My Savior Leads Me, Savior Like a Shepherd Lead Us, Joyful Joyful, We Adore Thee, *and* O Worship the King.

Special Music: *Special music could be presented by a choir, soloist, duet, or quartet. Selections could include* The Church Triumphant, God Leads Us Along, *and* Great Is Thy Faithfulness.

Hymn: *Selections could include* The Church's One Foundation, The Family of God, Blest Be the Tie, *and* Living For Jesus.

Special Recognitions: *Charter members, city officials, denominational officials, building committee members, architect, interior designer, contractor, and officials from the lending institution should all be recognized.*

Special Music: *Special music could be presented by a choir, soloists, duet, or quartet. Selections could be*

Come Holy Spirit, Give Me a Vision, Call for Reapers, *and* Seeking the Lost.

Suggested Sermon: *The minister is often asked to offici-ate building dedications; the building being dedicated could be a secular business, a missions center, a home-less shelter, a church building, etc. If he has time to de-liver a short lesson or sermon, he should focus on the place of this particular building in the kingdom of God, in the work of the church. The following is a sample that may be used for such an occasion, most fitting for the dedication of a ministry-oriented building.*

Christ's Church

Scripture: Matthew 16:13–20

Introduction: Our concept of the church should be founded on Bible truths. Far too often the model for the church is based on an educational, military, or corporate mode. The biblical mode emphasizes a family, fellowship, body, building, and bride.

1. The meaning which defines the church. What we call the church implies how we view it. The word *church* is used at least three ways in the New Testament. It is used to *designate the Lord's church* as the body of Christ, a build-ing, and a bride. These refer to what some call the invisible body of Christ. Every believer is member of the Lord's church. The term also *describes a local church.* In the epistles and Acts, writers refer to local churches in geo-graphical locations. Revelation 2—3 describe seven local churches in Asia Minor. The word may also *denote the larger church.* Acts 15 seems to use the word in this sense.

Apparently, not all the Corinthian believers met in the same geographical location but in homes scattered around the city.

2. The metaphors which describe the church. Paul uses the term *body* to describe the church. He reminds believers in Corinth that there is only one body but many members. He emphasizes the unity, unselfishness, and understanding of the body. Peter uses the term *building* to describe the church. Just as there is one building and yet many rooms in that building, so there is one church with many members. John uses the term *bride* to describe the church. Paul also uses this term to designate the nature of the church. The church will be adorned as a bride, beautiful, and blameless.

3. The ministries which denote the church. What is the church to do? The commission which Christ gave in the Gospels calls for *evangelism.* The church has the solemn responsibility and sufficient resources to share the gospel with all nations. Christ commission calls for the church to engage in *education.* Having shared the gospel, the church must teach those who have believed all the things which Christ taught. This is education. *Edification* remains a key component of the ministry of the church. Pastor-teachers have a unique responsibility to build up believers so they can effectively do the work of the ministry. *Equipping* the saints calls for the church's best effort. Believers need to be fully furnished so they can boldly do the work of the Lord. *Establishment* should be given a significant place in the ministry of the church. Believers need to be taught what they are to believe, why they believe it, and how to defend what they believe. *Encouragement* of believers is often overlooked in our attempt to reach others. Two of Paul's three missionary journeys were given to encouragement.

4. The message which distinguishes the church. The church has a unique message of *salvation, sanctification, separation, stewardship,* and *service.* The church's message is divinely revealed. It encompasses the entire responsibility of human beings.

5. The motivation which drives the church. The church is driven by two major motivating factors—love and loyalty. The greatest commandment is to love the Lord. Closely akin to love is loyalty. Throughout the Bible, great emphasis is given to loyalty and love as motivation for faithful service.

6. The membership which delineates the church. The church is made up of those who have been redeemed, those whose lives have been changed by the gospel. Church membership is incredibly important.

Conclusion: We need to review the biblical concept of the church so that every building dedicated to the work of God's kingdom and each person involved will fulfill its purpose to the glory of God. Christ will build His church and the gates of hell shall not prevail against it.

Act of Dedication

Minister: Brethren, Sisters, and Friends: We have assembled to dedicate this building to God as a place to be used for the sake of the gospel, as a place dedicated to the service of God and His eternal kingdom. To the glory of God our Father, to the honor of Jesus Christ, the Son of the living

God and our Lord and Savior; to the praise of the Holy
Spirit, source of life and light;

People: We dedicate this building.

Minister: The building and the people in it shall be dedicated to the service of the Lord; they shall live lives worthy
of the gospel to which they are called.

People: We dedicate this building.

*If the building is a church or specifically a building for
ministry, the following may be added:*

Minister: For missionary endeavor at home and abroad;
for world-wide evangelism and education, till all the kingdoms of the world become the kingdom of our Lord and of
His Christ; for the reform of social wrongs, till all human
society is transformed by the power of the gospel.

People: We dedicate this building.

Minister: In grateful remembrance of all who have loved
and served the kingdom; with hearts tender for those who
have departed from this earthly habitation; a free-will offering of thanksgiving and praise.

People: We dedicate this building.

Minister: Do you, now, give this building to God to be used
for the worship of God and for the up-building of His kingdom among men?

People: We do, in all sincerity, with love for God and faith in the Lord Jesus Christ.

Prayer of Dedication: *This prayer can be prayed by the minister, a deacon, or someone designated in advance. The congregation will join the minister after this prayer and say:*

"Even so, Lord Jesus! Glory to God for ever and ever. Amen."

Benediction: Now to Him who is able to do exceedingly abundantly above all that we ask or think, according to the power that works in us, to Him be glory in the church by Christ Jesus to all generations, forever and ever. Amen (Ephesians 3:20–21).

Now may the God of peace who brought up our Lord Jesus from the dead, that great Shepherd of the sheep, through the blood of the everlasting covenant, make you complete in every good work to do His will, working in you what is well pleasing in His sight, through Jesus Christ, to whom be glory forever and ever. Amen (Hebrews 13:20–21).

Home Dedication
By Dr. Melvin Worthington

A Sample Order of Service for a Home Dedication

Hymn

Scripture Reading

Charge

Prayer of Dedication

Benediction

A Sample Detailed Home Dedication Service

Hymn: *The minister shall read the words of appropriate hymns regarding the home. Selected hymns include* A Christian Home, Bless This House, Happy the Home Where God Is There, *and* Love at Home.

Scripture Reading: Now therefore, fear the LORD, serve Him in sincerity and in truth, and put away the gods which your fathers served on the other side of the River and in Egypt. Serve the LORD! And if it seems evil to you to serve the LORD, choose for yourselves this day whom you will serve, whether the gods which your fathers served that were on the other side of the River, or the gods of the Amorites, in whose land you dwell. But as for me and my house, we will serve the LORD." So the people answered and said: "Far be it from us that we should forsake the LORD to serve other gods; for the LORD our God is He who brought us and our fathers up out of the land of Egypt, from the house of bondage, who did those great signs in our sight, and preserved us in all the way that we went and among all the people through whom we passed. And the LORD drove out from before us all the people, including the Amorites who dwelt in the land. We also will serve the LORD, for He is our God" (Joshua 24:14–18).

Unless the LORD builds the house, they labor in vain who build it; unless the LORD guards the city, the watchman stays awake in vain. It is vain for you to rise up early, to sit up late, to eat the bread of sorrows; for so He gives His beloved sleep. Behold, children are a heritage from the LORD, the fruit of the womb is a reward. Like arrows in the hand of a warrior, so are the children of one's youth. Happy is the man who has his quiver full of them; they shall not be ashamed, but shall speak with their enemies in the gate (Psalm 127:1–5).

Wives, submit to your own husbands, as is fitting in the Lord. Husbands, love your wives and do not be bitter toward them. Children, obey your parents in all things, for this is well pleasing to the Lord. Fathers, do not provoke your children, lest they become discouraged (Colossians 3:18–21).

Charge

Minister: God has provided this beautiful house. This house is home for the family God has given you. Each family member who lives in this house has a unique role, responsibility, and relationship. Will each of you seek to find, follow, and finish God's will and with all your heart obey the precepts in God's Holy Word?

Family: We will, God being our Helper.

Minister: As God's steward will you acknowledge God's ownership of this house and promise to faithfully manage this house which God has entrusted to your care?

Family: We will, God being our Helper.

Prayer of Dedication: *The minister or a member of the family may pray the prayer of dedication.*

Benediction: Now may the God of peace Himself sanctify you completely; and may your whole spirit, soul, and body be preserved blameless at the coming of our Lord Jesus Christ. He who calls you is faithful, who also will do it. . . . The grace of our Lord Jesus Christ be with you. Amen (1 Thessalonians 5:23–24, 28).

Groundbreaking Service
By Dr. Melvin Worthington

A groundbreaking service is normally held on the property where a church or educational building is to be erected. Community leaders are often asked to attend this special service.

A Sample Order of Service for a Groundbreaking Service

Hymn	*Sermon*
Scripture Reading	*Breaking of Ground*
Prayer	*Hymn*
Special Recognitions	*Benediction*
Special Music	

A Sample Detailed Groundbreaking Service

Hymn: *Special selections that may be used include* How Firm a Foundation, The Church's One Foundation, A Glorious Church, I Love Thy Kingdom Lord, *and* The Family of God.

Scripture Reading: How lovely is Your tabernacle, O Lord of hosts! My soul longs, yes, even faints for the courts of the Lord; my heart and my flesh cry out for the living God. Even the sparrow has found a home, and the swallow a nest for herself, where she may lay her young—even Your altars, O Lord of hosts, my King and my God. Blessed are those who dwell in Your house; they will still be praising you. Selah. Blessed is the man whose strength is in You, whose heart is set on pilgrimage. As they pass through the Valley of Baca, they make it a spring; the rain also covers it with pools. They go from strength to strength; each one appears before God in Zion. O LORD God of hosts, hear my prayer; give ear, O God of Jacob! Selah. O God, behold our shield, and look upon the face of Your anointed. For a day in Your courts is better than a thousand. I would rather be a doorkeeper in the house of my God than dwell in the tents of wickedness. For the LORD God is a sun and shield; the Lord will give grace and glory; no good thing will He withhold from those who walk uprightly. O LORD of hosts, blessed is the man who trusts in You (Psalm 84:1–12)!

I was glad when they said to me. "Let us go into the house of the LORD." Our feet have been standing within your gates, O Jerusalem! Jerusalem is built as a city that is compact together, where the tribes go up, the tribes of the LORD, to the Testimony of Israel, to give thanks to the name of the Lord. For thrones are set there for judgment, the thrones of the house of David. Pray for the peace of Jerusalem: "May they prosper who love you. Peace be within your walls, prosperity within your palaces." For the sake of my brethren and companions, I will now say, "Peace be within you." Because of the house of the Lord our God I will seek your good (Psalm 122:1–9).

Prayer: *This prayer may be offered by the pastor, chairperson of the building committee, chairperson of the trustees, chairperson of the deacon board, or by someone designated prior to the service.*

Special Recognitions: *Construction company representatives, bank representatives—lending institution, city representatives, denominational representatives.*

Special Music: *Musical selections may be presented by a choir, duet, quartet, soloist or the entire congregation. Appropriate hymns include* Great Is Thy Faithfulness, A Mighty Fortress, The Family of God, The Church's One Foundation.

Sermon: *The suggested sermon for the building dedication service would be appropriate here too.*

Breaking of Ground

The minister or some designated person shall say:

We rejoice together as we break ground for a building to be erected for the glory of God. We pray that this spot will indeed be holy ground where we might find a burning bush of revelation and the benediction of Jehovah. Whereas we are constituted as a people of God—a local church and conscious of His commissioning us to be His ambassadors and witnesses, we therefore proceed, taking this first step in our building program. We will now turn the sod that here a building may be erected to His praise, a permanent witness to the people, a house of worship, a place for spiritual nourishment and inspiration as we grow together in Christ.

At this time designated individuals (usually three to five) will take a shovel in hand and turn a sizable piece of sod. The minister or designated person shall continue:

We have taken the first step toward the erection of our building. May the blessings of God be evident throughout the entire building process.

Hymn: *The assembled congregation could sing* Great Is Thy Faithfulness *or* Trust and Obey.

Benediction: Now may the God of peace Himself sanctify you completely; and may your whole spirit, soul, and body be preserved blameless at the coming of our Lord Jesus Christ. He who calls you is faithful, who also will do it (1 Thessalonians 5:23–24).

Installation/Consecration Service
By Dr. Melvin Worthington

A Sample Order of Service for Installation/ Consecration for Service

The order and form for installation/consecration for service varies for place to place. The following is a general order that incorporates basic principles and precepts regarding the service.

This order of installation may be used during a regular Sunday morning or evening worship service or some other appropriate time.

Prelude

Hymn

Special Music

Scripture Reading

Hymn

Special Music

Sermon

Act of Installation/Consecration

Prayer of Installation/Consecration

Hymn

Benediction

A Sample Detailed Installation/ Consecration Service

Prelude: *The musicians should play appropriate music dealing with Christian commitment and service. Suggested selections include* I'd Rather Have Jesus, I'll Go Where You Want Me to Go, If Jesus Goes With Me, Wherever He Leads, I'll Go, *and* Now I Belong to Him.

Hymn: *Suggested selections include* Give Me a Vision, A Call for Reapers, The Old Rugged Cross, I Love to Tell the Story, I Am Happy in the Service of the King, *and* Trust and Obey.

Special Music: *Special music could be presented by a choir, soloist, duet, or quartet. Suggested selections include* I'll Go Where You Want Me to Go, All for Jesus, Great Is Thy Faithfulness, *and* Until Then.

Scripture Reading: You therefore, my son, be strong in the grace that is in Christ Jesus. And the things that you have heard from me among many witnesses, commit these to faithful men who will be able to teach others also. You therefore must endure hardship as a good soldier of Jesus Christ. No one engaged in warfare entangles himself with the affairs of this life, that he may please him who enlisted him as a soldier. And also if anyone competes in athletics, he is not crowned unless he competes according to the rules. . . . Be diligent to present yourself approved to God, a worker who does not need to be ashamed, rightly dividing the word of truth. But shun profane and idle babblings, for they will increase to more ungodliness. . . . Flee also youthful lusts; but pursue righteousness, faith, love, peace with those who call on the Lord out of a pure heart. But avoid foolish and ignorant disputes, knowing that they generate strife. And a servant of the Lord must not quarrel but be gentle to all, able to teach, patient, in humility correcting those who are in opposition, if God perhaps will grant them repentance, so that they may know the truth, and that they may come to their senses and escape the snare of the devil, having been taken captive by him to do his will (2 Timothy 2:1–5; 15–16; 22–26).

Let a man so consider us, as servants of Christ and stewards of the mysteries of God. Moreover it is required in stewards that one be found faithful. But with me it is a very small thing that I should be judged by you or by a human court. In fact, I do not even judge myself. For I know of nothing against myself, yet I am not justified by this; but He who judges me is the Lord. Therefore judge nothing before the time, until the Lord comes, who will bring to light the hidden things of darkness and reveal the counsels of the hearts. Then each one's praise will come from God (1 Corinthians 4:1–5).

Now great multitudes went with Him. And He turned and said to them, "If anyone comes to Me and does not hate his father and mother, wife and children, brothers and sisters, yes, and his own life also, he cannot be My disciple. And whoever does not bear his cross and come after Me cannot be My disciple. For which of you, intending to build a tower, does not sit down first and count the cost, whether he has enough to finish it—lest, after he has laid the foundation, and is not able to finish, all who see it begin to mock him, saying, 'This man began to build and was not able to finish.' Or what king, going to make war against another king, does not sit down first and consider whether he is able with ten thousand to meet him who comes against him with twenty thousand? Or else, while the other is still a great way off, he sends a delegation and asks conditions of peace. So likewise, whoever of you does not forsake all that he has cannot be My disciple. Salt is good; but if the salt has lost its flavor, how shall it be seasoned? It is neither fit for the land nor for the dunghill, but men throw it out. He who has ears to hear, let him hear!" (Luke 14:25–35).

Sermon—Found Faithful

Scripture: 1 Corinthians 4:1–5; 2 Timothy 2; Luke 14:15–25

Introduction: Faithfulness is a virtue which characterizes those who serve the Lord. Faithfulness requires dedication, discernment, and determination as well as discipline. Fidelity in face of corrupt contemporary situations is not an easy task. Charles Hodge was correct when he declared, "The great requisite for the discharge of the office of a steward is fidelity. As his is a servant he must be faithful to his Master. The application of this to the case of ministers is plain. Fidelity to Christ as servants; not currogating to themselves any other than ministerial power, or venturing to go beyond His commands. Fidelity to the truths which God has revealed, nor mixing these truths with their own speculations, must less substituting for those doctrines human knowledge or wisdom."

1. To be found faithful we must go. Jonah was instructed to go to Ninevah and cry against that wicked city. Isaiah heard God's call to go and responded by saying, "Here am I, send me." Obedient Christians have always been ready to go do the Master's bidding. Those who would go must hear God's call, consent to obey that call and accept the commission of that call. God has this intelligent, individual, and indispensable requirement of service if we would be found faithful. No one may go for us. Each must go for himself.

2. To be found faithful we must give. Giving one's time, talent, tithe, and testimony is a natural dimension of the obedient servant. The spirit of giving rather than getting enables one to cheerfully implement the go element which God requires. Time must be set aside for the Lord's work. Talent must be redirected. The tithe must be considered a minimum. All our treasures must be at God's disposal. A ready testimony accompanies those who look to give, not to get.

3. To be found faithful we must grow. Growth is as much God's divine plan for His children as is going and giving. The development process is planned by God along with the diet to prompt it. Dwarfed development contributes to Christian worker casualties. It is only avoided by dogged grow-or-die determination. Growth in one's Christian experience is never an accident, but the result of careful attention to God's prescribed plan.

4. To be found faithful we must be on guard. The Christian worker must be on guard lest he stray under the influence of false teachers. Peter exhorts that we "beware" lest we land in the error of the wicked and fall. John exhorts to "try the spirits." Paul warns Timothy of dangerous trends in the last times when some will depart from the faith. Believers are cautioned lest when we have preached and taught others we ourselves become castaways. Sound doctrine, saintly deportment and spiritual development only come to those who take God seriously in the matter of guarding against personal error, those who offer no excuses for the sordid lives of others, but who at the same time reject anything less than their best for God.

5. To be found faithful we must glorify. One requirement for being found faithful is glorifying our Heavenly Father. Christians are not just to be faithful but "to be found" or discovered faithful. As cold as the judge and the critic may be, even they soon acknowledge when a child of God is the genuine article. And they do know the difference. Joseph Parker said, " . . . the whole diary of the man's actions is regarded in its unity; and the result is that the man has been discovered to be faithful, found to be faithful, as the result of a prolonged, critical, unsparing scrutiny: then the printed testimonial may be burned, the testimony of friends is no longer required; the man has proved himself faithful."

Conclusion: There is only one thing that produces faithfulness on the order that God requires. Genius is not the building block of faithfulness, nor is gift or amiability. God only builds on character—pristine character and sterling integrity.

Act of Installation/Consecration

Minister: In precept and practice you will be constantly influencing those entrusted to your care in the deepest things of life—eternal things. Will you be faithful, earnest, sympathetic, and preserving, keeping in mind that the goals of Christian ministry included evangelism, education, edification, encouragement, equipping, and establishing others in the faith?

Candidate: I will, the Lord being my Helper.

Minister: Inasmuch as you have been called to this ministry, will you endeavor, God being your helper, to discharge faithfully its duties? Will you be diligent in your study of the scriptures and dedicated in serving the Lord Jesus Christ?

Candidate: I will, the Lord being my Helper.

Minister: Today we have witnessed the pledge of this candidate/candidates. As a church, will you be faithful in prayer and support of the efforts of this candidate?

Congregation: We will, the Lord being our Helper.

Prayer of Installation/Consecration: *This prayer may be prayed by the minister or someone designated prior to the service.*

Hymn: *Hymns which could be selected include* I'll Go Where You Want Me to Go, All for Jesus, Am I a Soldier of the Cross, If Jesus Goes With Me I'll Go Anywhere, *and* Anywhere with Jesus I Can Safely Go.

Benediction: May God bless you in the responsibilities you are about to assume and make you fruitful in all your service. May you be a faithful steward over these few things, that in the end you may be made ruler over many things. And may the church be prospered and its great Head be honored by your fidelity. Amen.

Now to Him who is able to establish you according to my gospel and the preaching of Jesus Christ, according to the revelation of the mystery kept secret since the world began but now has been made manifest, and by the prophetic Scriptures has been made known to all nations, according to the commandment of the everlasting God, for obedience to the faith—to God, alone wise, be glory through Jesus Christ forever. Amen (Romans 16:25–27).

Now to Him who is able to keep you from stumbling, and to present you faultless before the presence of His glory with exceeding joy, to God our Savior, Who alone is wise, be glory and majesty, dominion and power, both now and forever. Amen (Jude 24–25).

Ordination of Ministers
By Dr. Melvin Worthington

Sample Order of Service for the Ordination of a Minister

Prelude	*Ministry of Music*
Hymn	*Ordination Message*
Prayer	*Presentation of the Bible*
Scripture Reading	*Ministry of Music*
Ordination Charge	*Benediction*
Prayer of Ordination	*Postlude*

Sample Ordination of Ministers Service

Prelude: *The organist and pianist should play appropriate music related to Christian service.*

Hymn: *Some hymns which are appropriate include:* My Jesus, I Love Thee, I Am Happy in the Service of the King, All for Jesus, I Will Go Where You Want Me to Go.

Prayer

Scripture Reading: Now the Spirit expressly says that in the latter times some will depart from the faith, giving heed to deceiving spirits and doctrines of demons, speaking lies in hypocrisy, having their own conscience seared with a hot iron, forbidding to marry, and commanding to abstain from foods which God created to be received with thanksgiving by those who believe and know the truth. For every creature of God is good, and nothing is to be refused if it is received with thanksgiving; for it is sanctified by the word of God and prayer. If you instruct the brethren in these things, you will be a good minister of Jesus Christ, nourished in the words of faith and of the good doctrine which you have carefully followed. But reject profane and old wives fables, and exercise yourself toward godliness. For bodily exercise profits a little, but godliness is profitable for all things, having promise of the life that now is and of that which is to come. This is a faithful saying and worthy of all acceptance. For to this end we both labor and suffer reproach, because we trust in the living God, who is the Savior of all men, especially of those who believe. These things command and teach. Let no one despise your youth, but be an example to the believers in word, in conduct, in love, in spirit, in faith, in purity. Till I come, give attention to reading, to exhortation, to doctrine. Do not neglect the gift that is in you, which was given to you by prophecy with the laying on of the hands of the eldership. Meditate on these things; give yourself entirely to them, that your progress may be evident to all. Take heed to yourself and to the doctrine. Continue in them, for in doing this you will save both yourself and those who hear you (1 Timothy 4:1–16).

When the appointed time for the ordination has arrived, the candidate having satisfied all the requirements for ordination, the chairman will state the purpose of the meeting and make such remarks as may be appropriate and ask the candidate the following questions.

Question: Do you accept the Bible as God's inspired, infallible, inerrant, immutable, indestructible, and indispensable Word?

Answer: I do, the Lord being my Helper.

Question: Do you understand the requirements, responsibilities and realities that are about to be place upon you by being ordained and set apart as an ambassador of the Lord Jesus Christ?

Answer: I do, the Lord being my Helper.

Question: Are you ready and willing to accept and assume the responsibility to peruse, preach, and practice God's Word with boldness; to minister to the needs of those to whom you are sent without partiality, and to give yourself sacrificially and without reserve to the educating, edification, and equipping of the body of Christ?

Answer: I am, the Lord being my Helper.

Question: Will you endeavor to be diligent in the study of God's Word; instant and faithful in prayer, an example in Christian piety and discipline before your people and the community, in order that your life may be a worthy Christian example and that upon your ministry the blessing of God may rest?

Answer: I will, the Lord being my Helper.

Question: Recognizing the sacred responsibility of your call and aware of your own human weakness, will you seek the leadership and empowerment of the Holy Spirit in order that you may be a faithful minister of Him who has called you?

Answer: I will, the Lord being my Helper.

Ordination Charge

I charge you to pursue the Word of God. Paul charged Timothy, "Till I come, give attention to reading, to exhortation, to doctrine.... Meditate on these things; give yourself entirely to them, that your progress may be evident to all" (1 Timothy 4:13,15). Paul further charged Timothy to, "Be diligent to present yourself approved to God, a worker who does not need to be ashamed, rightly dividing the word of truth" (2 Timothy 2:15).

I charge you to practice the Word of God. Paul affirms this when he says, "This is a faithful saying: If a man desires the position of a bishop, he desires a good work. A bishop then must be blameless, the husband of one wife, temperate, sober-minded, of good behavior, hospitable, able to teach; not given to wine, not violent, not greedy for money, but gentle, not quarrelsome, not covetous; one who rules his own house well, having his children in submission with all reverence (for if a man does not know how to rule his own house, how will he take care of the church of God?); not a novice, lest being puffed up with pride he fall into the same condemnation as the devil. Moreover he must have a good testimony among those who are outside, lest he fall into reproach and the snare of the devil . . . Let no man despise your youth, but be an example of the believers in word, in conduct, in love, in spirit, in faith, in purity. . . . Flee also youthful lusts; but pursue righteousness, faith, love, peace with those who call on the Lord out of a pure heart. But avoid foolish and ignorant disputes, knowing that they generate strife. And a servant of the Lord must not quarrel but be gentle to all, able to teach, patient, in humility correcting those who are in opposition, if God perhaps will grant them repentance, so that they may know the truth, and that they may come to their senses and escape the snare of the devil, having been taken captive by him to do his will" (1 Timothy 3:1–7; 4:12; 2 Timothy 2:22–26).

I charge you to preach the Word of God. You are called to be a preacher. Some assume the call to preach and do very little about it, becoming entangled with various professions of the world and their ministry becomes a *side-line*. I believe it is proper to include in this charge that if you are called to be a preacher then be a preacher. You are not called to be a politician, schoolteacher, a businessman, or a social worker—you are a man of God called to preach. Paul's final instruction to Timothy was, "I charge you therefore before God and the Lord Jesus Christ, who will judge the living and the dead at His appearing and His kingdom: Preach the word! Be ready in season and out of season. Convince, rebuke, exhort, with all longsuffering and teaching. For the time will come when they will not endure sound doctrine, but according to their own desires, because they have itching ears, they will heap up for themselves teachers; and they will turn their ears away from the truth, and be turned aside to fables. But you be watchful in all things, endure afflictions, do the work of an evangelist, fulfill your ministry" (2 Timothy 4:1–5).

Prayer of Ordination: *The candidate shall kneel and be joined by all ordained ministers present who shall place* *their hands upon him. The Prayer of Ordination is offered by someone previously selected.*

Ministry of Music: *Appropriate music can be rendered by a choir, quartet, duet, congregation, or solo.*

Ordination Sermon—*The Profile of a Pastor*

Scripture: 1 Timothy 3, 4; 2 Timothy 2, 4; Titus 1

Introduction: The Lord exercised special care for His church by appointing pastors. The pastoral ministry is not an afterthought with God, but a divine, designated, and designed office which meets the needs of the church. The pastoral office demands a uniquely qualified individual, equipped with proper credentials. He must possess good, natural, and acquired abilities, deep and ardent piety, be especially called of God to the work, and ordained by prayer and laying on of hands. Proper credentials which are prescribed by the Scriptures enable a pastor to preach the Word, administer the ordinances, visit the flock, and perform the duties of a faithful minister.

1. His personal credentials. The pastor must be a *godly man,* possessing and practicing the Christian virtues. He should be a man of irreproachable character demonstrating truth, honesty, and general uprightness. He must be a *gentle man.* Paul reminds Timothy that the servant of the Lord must not strive but be gentle to all men. Gentleness is not a sign of weakness but a necessary ingredient for the pastor who, without it, is lacking in sound personal credentials. The godly pastor is a *gracious man.* Pastors must manifest sensitivity and sensibility as they perform the work of the pastoral office. The gracious man is a helpful man.

2. His public credentials. The profile of a pastor includes his public credentials. He must have the reputation of a man of integrity among those who are not Christians if he is to reach them. A pastor's public testimony is his passport behind closed doors in the community. Albert Barnes aptly warns, "It is impossible for a minister to overestimate the importance of having a fair character in the view of the world, and no man should be introduced into the ministry or sustained in it that has not a fair reputation." No amount of ability, accomplishment, achievement, or activity will substitute in the eyes of the lost for the moral integrity of the pastor. Without integrity he is penniless in a world of towering needs.

3. His practical credentials. The pastor *superintends* the local church. He is not to arrogantly dictate to the congregation, but lead them in the ways of God and take the oversight (1 Peter 5:2). The pastor *shepherds* the flock, watches lovingly over them, and serves the local church. There is no contradiction when the pastor is charged to both superintend and serve. The greatest in the kingdom is still a servant. The pastor *speaks* to his congregation; he is a preacher and teacher. His responsibility is to preach and pray. He speaks to the saints from the Word of God and speaks to the Sovereign in prayer about the saints. The good pastor will be characterized as a *student* of the Word of God. A call to pastor includes the call to study (2 Timothy 2:15). The pastor is a *soldier.* He leads his congregation in battle. His courage, consecration, consistency, and concerns are manifested in those who follow him. He fights the good fight of faith, follows the Lord Jesus, and flees the entanglements of this world. He organizes, operates, and observes his congregation in their constant warfare. The pastor is a *sensitive* man. No one should be more sensitive to the needs and problems of people than he. He is not arrogant or abrasive. He laughs with his congregation and weeps with them. He is genuinely interested in the people. No problem of need is insignificant. The pastor is a *separated* man. All who fill the pastoral office must understand that they are unique. They are distinctive, and therefore the highest level of dedication and separation must characterize their lives. Lack of biblical separation by pastors has brought disgrace to many churches. No man dare enter the ministry until he has settled the separation question for himself. The pastor is a *strong* man. When others are filled with despair, discouragement, and disappointment, he demonstrates a strength which is not humanly possible apart from a daily dependence on the Lord. He is not given to emotional highs and lows. He is steadfast and consistent. The pastor is a *sensible* man. He has the ability to carefully, cautiously and compassionately view the work of the pastoral office. He has been given a large measure of *common sense.*

4. His professional credentials. Consider the pastor's professional credentials. Whether local church or ordaining council be charged with the responsibility for ordaining ministers, it is evident that these must be approved by their peers and parishioners. The Scriptures teach the principle of *accountability.* Every minister must be accountable for his doctrine and deportment, not only to God but to those who ordained him. The pastor needs *acceptability* from his peers and parishioners. Paul was accepted by the disciples in Jerusalem. Acceptability is necessary for effective ministry in any group. The pastor must sense that he is *appreciated*. Churches are to esteem their pastors highly for their work.

Conclusion: The pastor-teacher is a divine gift to the church. Most writers believe the pastor is one individual with a two-fold ministry. Those who *tend* the flock must also *teach* the flock. The ideal pastor engages in a didactic ministry, feeding the saints on expository preaching, giving them the rich food of the Word, thereby prompting the church's internal development, discernment, and dedication which leads to numerical growth as well.

Presentation of the Bible: *The candidate is presented a Bible. It should be a good study Bible.*

Ministry in Music: *Appropriate music can be rendered by a choir, quartet, solo, duet, or the congregation.*

Benediction: Now to Him who is able to establish you according to my gospel and the preaching of Jesus Christ, according to the revelation of the mystery kept secret since the world began but now made manifest, and by the prophetic Scriptures has been made known to all nations, according to the commandment of the everlasting God, for obedience to the faith—to God, alone wise, be glory through Jesus Christ forever. Amen (Romans 16:25–27).

Postlude: *The organist and pianist should play appropriate music related to Christian service.*

Ordination of Deacons
By Dr. Melvin Worthington

Sample Ordination of Deacon
Order of Service

The ordination service for a deacon may be a part of any duly called public service of the congregation at the discretion of the minister who shall officiate at the service.

Prelude	*Ordination Charge*
Hymn	*Ordination Prayer*
Prayer	*Hymn*
Scripture Reading	*Benediction*
Ministry of Music	*Postlude*
Ordination Sermon	

Sample Detailed Service for Ordination of a Deacon

The ordination service for a deacon may be a part of any duly called public service (regular church service) of the congregation at the discretion of the minister who shall officiate at the service.

Prelude: *Organist and pianist should play music appropriate for Christian service. Appropriate hymns could include* Near the Cross, The Old Rugged Cross, Here Am I, Send Me, My Jesus I Love Thee, *and* In the Service of the King.

Hymn: Grace Greater Than Our Sin, Great Is Thy Faithfulness, *and* Breathe on Me *are hymns which could be used.*

Scripture Reading: Now in those days, when the number of the disciples was multiplying, there arose a complaint against the Hebrews by the Hellenists, because their widows were neglected in the daily distribution. Then the twelve summoned the multitude of the disciples and said "It is not desirable that we should leave the word of God and serve tables. Therefore, brethren, seek out from among you seven men of good reputation, full of the Holy Spirit and wisdom, whom we may appoint over this business; but we will give ourselves continually to prayer and to the ministry of the word." And the saying pleased the whole multitude. And they chose Stephen, a man full of faith and the Holy Spirit, and Philip, Prochorus, Nicanor, Timon, Parmenas, and Nicolas, a proselyte from Antioch, whom they set before the apostles; and when they had prayed, they laid hands on them. Then the word of God spread, and the number of disciples multiplied greatly in Jerusalem, and a great many of the priests were obedient to the faith (Acts 6:1–7).

Likewise deacons must be reverent, not double-tongued, not given to much wine, not greedy for money, holding the mystery of the faith with a pure conscience. But let these also first be tested; then let them serve as deacons, being found blameless. Likewise, their wives must be reverent, not slanderers, temperate, faithful in all things. Let deacons be the husbands of one wife, ruling their children and their own houses well. For those who have served well as deacons obtain for themselves a good standing and great boldness in the faith which is in Christ Jesus (1 Timothy 3:8–13).

***Ministry of Music:** Appropriate special music by a choir, quartet, duet, solo, or the congregation relating to Christian service could be utilized at this point in the service.*

Ordination Sermon—*The Deacon's Duties*

Scriptures: Act 6:1–7; 1 Timothy 3:8–13

Introduction: Deacons are ordained by the local church to minister to the congregation and exercise general spiritual leadership. They assist the pastor in administering the ordinances, and may have to conduct worship services in the pastor's absence. Deacons should meet the biblical criteria set forth in Acts 6:1–7 and 1 Timothy 3:8–13. The ministry of the Lord Jesus Christ was characterized by His concern for the physical and spiritual needs of those who heard Him. The early church shared His concern and chose deacons to this ministry. The deacon becomes the heart and hand of the church in seeking out and ministering to needs of those within and without the church.

1. The office of the deacon. The *concept of deacons* is disclosed in Acts 6:1–7. The *choice of deacons* is denoted in Acts 6:1–7. The *credentials for deacons* are detailed in 1 Timothy 3:8–13 and Acts 6:1–7. The *companions of deacons* are directed in 1 Timothy 3:11.

2. The obligation of the deacon. The deacon has a unique *role, relationship, and responsibility* to the minister and membership of the church in which he serves. The deacon's obligation includes *leadership, lecturing, listening, and laboring.* Deacons should possess sound piety, good business capacity, and large benevolence; they should be ordained by prayer and the laying on of hands by the presbytery; they hold office at the pleasure of the church during the maintenance of Christian character, faithful service, and sound doctrine; they assist at baptism and the Lord's Supper, have care of the poor, and conduct religious meetings in the absence of the pastor.

3. The opportunities of the deacon. The first deacons were appointed in order to serve tables and enable the apostles to give themselves continually to prayer and the ministry of the Word. Deacons have the opportunity to *serve the membership, support the minister, and share the message.*

Conclusion: The office, obligation, and opportunities of a deacon are clearly, concisely, and carefully recorded in Holy Scripture in Acts 6 and 1 Timothy 3. Following the precedent thus established by the early church, with the advice and approval of the apostles, the brethren of this congregation have desired men of honest report and full of the Holy Spirit and wisdom, chosen from among themselves, to serve as deacons. We are gathered together today to ordain brethren as deacons.

Candidates for ordination should come forward at this point and stand before the minister who will give the charge.

Ordination Charge: My brother/brethren, you have been elected by the vote of this church, to serve in the capacity of a deacon.

Question: My brother/brethren, this church has voted upon you an honor, and a great responsibility, in selecting you to the office of deacon. Will you accept this responsibility and strive to fill the position to which are called, and to promote the interest of the church, to assist the pastor whenever you can do so, and to look out for the poor and needy of the church, seeing that none shall suffer for material aid, so far as is in your power to prevent?

Answer: I will, the Lord being my Helper.

Question: Will you affirm your allegiance to Christ, the church, and the Scriptures?

Answer: I will, the Lord being my Helper.

Question: Will you accept the office of deacon in this church, and promise faithfully to perform the duties required in this office?

Answer: I will, the Lord being my Helper.

Question: Will you promise to cooperate with the pastor and to further the interests of this church in promoting its harmonious and effective working of all its ministries?

Answer: I will, the Lord being my Helper.

The minister asks the congregation the following question:

Question: Will you, the members of the church, acknowledge and affirm this brother as a deacon? Will you esteem him, encourage him, and cooperate with him as he performs the duties of a deacon?

Answer: We will, the Lord being our Helper.

At this point the minister will take the candidate by the hand both standing and deliver the following charge.

I now charge you, in the name of the Father, and of the Son, and of the Holy Ghost, that you ever strive to fill your office to the best of you knowledge, and that you will seek divine guidance in all of your work.

The candidate will kneel; the minister, and all ordained deacons holding membership in the church will lay hands on the candidate.

Ordination Prayer: *This prayer may be prayed by the minister or the chairman of the deacon board.*

Hymn: *The congregation will sing an appropriate hymn emphasizing Christian service.*

Benediction

Postlude: *The organist and pianist will play an appropriate hymn emphasizing Christian service.*

Baptism and the Lord's Supper

◆

A Baptism Service for Professing Adults and Children

By Rev. Todd Kinde

Sample Order of Service for a Baptism

Prelude

Hymn of Praise

Opening Prayer

The Meaning of Baptism

Hymn of Focus

Presentation of Candidate(s)

Baptismal Vows

Affirmation of Faith

Words of Institution

Prayer of Thanksgiving

Testimonies and Baptisms

Remembering Your Baptism

Songs of Renewal

Benediction

Sample Detailed Baptism Service

Prelude

Hymn of Praise

Opening Prayer: Lord, may we who are baptized into the death of Jesus Christ continue to put to death our sinful desires. And may we pass from death to resurrection life through the work of Him who died, was buried, and rose again for us, Your Son our Savior Christ Jesus.

The Meaning of Baptism: Baptism is a holy ordinance/ sacrament appointed by Christ as a rite of passage into the fellowship of the redeemed community, His church. Jesus Christ spoke to His disciples commissioning them, saying: "All authority has been given to Me in heaven and on earth. Go therefore and make disciples of all the nations, baptizing them in the name of the Father and of the Son and of the Holy Spirit, teaching them to observe all things that I have commanded you; and lo, I am with you always, even to the end of the age." Amen (Matthew 28:18–20).

The ordinance/sacrament of baptism is a sign of new birth by the Holy Spirit; union with Christ in His death, burial, and resurrection; union with His church; single devotion to Jesus as Lord; and the start of a new life in Christ.

Hymn of Focus: *Baptized in Water* (Words: Hope Publishing Co.); *I Pledge Allegiance to the Lamb* (1994 Word Music, Inc.)

Presentation of Baptismal Candidate(s): I present *Name(s)* for baptism.

Baptismal Vows: *The early church made vows at the time of baptism. In the vows the candidates renounce all that is evil and then embrace the love and loyalty of Christ. The pastor addresses the candidates who then answer. These vows can be made individually or together as a group.*

Minister: Do you turn away from Satan and all the spiritual forces of evil that rebel against God?

Candidate(s): I turn away from them.

Minister: Do you turn away from all sinful desires that draw you from fellowship with God?

Candidate(s): I turn away from them.

Minister: Do you turn to Jesus Christ?

Candidate(s): Yes! I am trusting Jesus Christ as my Lord and Savior.

Minister: Do you intend to be a faithful follower of Christ, serving Him by obeying His Word and showing His saving grace in your life?

Candidate(s): Yes, with the Lord's help.

Minister: Do you promise to devote yourself to the apostle's teaching and the to the fellowship, to the breaking of bread, and to the prayers?

Candidate(s): I promise, with the Lord's help.

Affirmation of Faith: *The Apostle's Creed in the form of three questions and answers has been used at Christian baptisms since as early as the third century. The creed gives the essential content of the Christian faith, which is to be appropriated and affirmed by all believers. Some congregations may choose to omit "He descended into hell" for theological reasons. The pastor addresses everyone present at the service. The congregation along with the candidates respond.*

Minister: Do you believe in God the Father?

Congregation: I believe in God, the Father Almighty, Maker of heaven and earth.

Minister: Do you believe in Jesus Christ?

Congregation: I believe in Jesus Christ, His only Son, our Lord: who was conceived by the Holy Spirit, and born of the virgin Mary. He suffered under Pontius Pilate, was crucified, died, and was buried. He descended into hell; the third day He rose again from the dead; He ascended to heaven and is seated at the right hand of God the Father Almighty. From there He will come to judge the living and the dead.

Minister: Do you believe in the Holy Spirit?

Congregation: I believe in the Holy Spirit, the holy church, the communion of saints, the forgiveness of sins, the resurrection of the body, and the life everlasting. Amen.

Words of Institution: *The pastor moves to the baptistery or font. A pitcher of water may be held as the pastor says,*

The promises of God's grace are signed and sealed to us in our baptism. God has promised to forgive our sin, to adopt us into His household, and to send His Holy Spirit to make us holy. These promises are made visible in the water of baptism.

(The pitcher of water may be poured into the baptistery or font.)

Prayer of Thanksgiving: *A prayer thanking the Triune God for His work of salvation, sanctification, and glorification may be offered at this time. The prayer should also include the petition that God would honor the sac-*

rament/ordinance in which the candidates are about to participate and the congregation witness.

Testimonies and Baptisms: *The pastor will enter the baptistery or approach the font. The first candidate will then join the pastor. The candidates may wear white robes, which represent the righteousness of Christ. The pastor will ask the candidate to give a testimony of saving faith in Christ. The testimony should include the means by which the candidate came to receive the gospel and the people instrumental in that process. A Scripture verse, which gives assurance of God's salvation and faithfulness, could also be included in the testimony.*

The pastor may make a cross sign using his thumb gently on the candidate's forehead saying,

Name, I baptize you in the name of the Father and of the Son and of the Holy Spirit. Amen.

Baptism by immersion may be done forward so as to kneel in humility before the Lord or backward to symbolize the death, burial, and resurrection. A white cloth or handkerchief may be used to cover the candidate's face before immersing in the water.

Forward Immersion: Candidate will place palms together. Pastor will grasp the candidate's wrists with one hand and place the other hand on candidate's back, supporting it. Pastor will assist candidate to kneel in the water and then bow forward until the water covers candidate (a small stool may be placed in the baptistery to allow the candidate to sit rather than kneel). Pastor will assist candidate in rising from the water. This movement should be gentle and steady but not fast.

Backward Immersion: Candidate will place palms together. Pastor will grasp candidate's wrists with one hand, supporting candidate with the other arm. Pastor will tip candidate backwards, as the candidate bends knees, thus assisting in the process (a small stool may be placed in the baptistery to allow the candidate to sit). As the candidate proceeds backward the candidate should raise his/her hands to his/her face and clasp his/her nose as entering the water. Pastor will assist the candidate upward to his/her feet. This movement should be gentle and steady but not fast.

If a baptismal font is used, the candidate will kneel at the font and the pastor will pour or sprinkle water on his/her head.

After either mode of baptism, the pastor will lay hands on the newly baptized person and pray a blessing over him/her:

The blessing of the Triune God, Father, Son, and Holy Spirit, descend upon you and dwell in you forever. Amen.

Those who have been immersed will proceed from the baptistery, wrapped in a large white bath towel and escorted to a room to dry and change clothing.

Remembering Your Baptism: *After all candidates have been baptized, the pastor may invite those of the congregation who have already been baptized to remember their baptism. Some may not have made vows at their*

*own baptism but seeing and hearing them at this service
desire to do so now. Some may have neglected the life of
holiness and want to renew their vows to the Lord. After
explaining this time of renewal the pastor may say,*

Water cleanses and refreshes; Jesus Christ is the Living
Water. Through baptism Christ calls us to love, to trust,
and to obey God completely; to die to sin and the world;
and to live a holy life in Christ Jesus.

I invite you to remember God's promise in baptism today, to turn away from evil, and to reaffirm your loyalty to
Jesus Christ and your commitment to His church.

*The people may stand around the baptistery or font to
touch the water and to pray quietly or in silence.*

Songs of Renewal: *Songs may be sung during this time
of reflection as people gather around the baptistery or
font.*

Benediction: *The pastor will ask the congregation to
stand as the blessing is pronounced.*

"The grace of the Lord Jesus Christ, and the love of God,
and the communion of the Holy Spirit be with you all.
Amen" (2 Corinthians 13:14).

Baptism Sermon
By Rev. Todd Kinde

Dead Center

Scripture: 1 Peter 3:13—4:2

Introduction: We all have a tendency to lose focus and direction, wading hopelessly in a sea of activity without real purpose. Perhaps you have been searching, looking for something to keep your life from being meaningless as you spin dizzily in a life that seems to have no eternal significance. Your life has no center. Perhaps in an attempt to find meaning you make a hobby or career central to your being and identity. Sooner or later you will be disappointed with whatever worldly thing is at the center of your life. Life continues to spin out of control when there is no true center to your being.

The solution to your wandering is submission to Christ. First Peter 3:13—4:6 describes a life with Christ at dead center. Jesus is Lord of all. As Lord he is to be the center of your being. In your hearts you are to set apart Christ as Lord. To set apart in the Bible means to take something from the periphery and put it in the center.

1. When Christ is the center of our being we are people of hope (3:13–17). Peter reminds us that we are blessed who have trusted the Lord Jesus Christ as Savior from our sin and Lord of our life. It is true that suffering in all probability will accompany the Christian life. We will suffer for bearing testimony to Christ and the kind of character that is His. Suffering here and now is temporal and should be understood as such. Blessing is eternal and as such it is obvious that our suffering now for the sake of Christ is really not to our harm. So do not fear what the world fears. Our hope is in Christ. We need not fear the wrath of God, for we have trusted in His Word. Death and destruction are nothing to us, for the God we serve is able to bring life out of death.

Since Christ is central to your being you will be ready and more than willing to share of the hope you have in Christ Jesus our Lord. Timidity and shyness will be pushed away as the hope of Christ comes rushing through your being and out your life. But this will always be done in the character of Christ's submissive spirit—with gentleness and respect. You will speak the truth with love. When Christ is central you will give the reason for the hope you have in Christ, the hope of eternity with God. You have peace with God and no longer fear the wrath of God.

2. When Christ is the center of our being we are dead to sin (3:18–22). To testify will mean that some attitudes are going to need changing. Fear and pride must be eradicated. Because of our sinfulness the only way to rid ourselves of fear and pride is to die. We must die to sin and to self. To do this we must identify with the death of Jesus our Lord. Christ suffered in His body. His suffering was to pay what you owed God for your sin and to satisfy the anger of God over your sin. Jesus was without sin, a perfect person, indeed, God in the flesh. It is only a perfect person who could pay the penalty: the righteous for the unrighteous. Christ suffered and died once for all. It cannot be repeated ever again for all eternity, nor does it need to be. God the Father raised the Son to life anew by the power of the Spirit. The Spirit gives life.

Jesus said, "as it was in the days of Noah, so it will be also in the days of the Son of Man" (Luke 17:26; Matthew

24:37). Peter here says basically the same thing. The gospel was preached to the world in the days of Noah before the flood. God waited patiently, 120 years, while Noah built the ark. During that time Noah preached with a hammer in his hand (2 Peter 2:5; Hebrews 11:7). This brief statement recalls everything that is in Genesis 6. One hundred and twenty years of preaching resulted in rejection of the message. Eight souls, however, were saved through the water, Noah's family. What about your family? Have you testified of God's salvation to your family?

Peter says this floodwater is a symbol of baptism, which now saves you. It is a baptism not merely of water that washes dirt off your body, but a baptism with Christ. Christ refers to His death as a baptism (Mark 10:32–45; Luke 12:50). When we are converted we are baptized into Christ's death. We die to sin and self. The ordinance of water baptism is a symbol of that inner regeneration that took place.

Paul in states in Romans,

> How shall we who died to sin live any longer in it? Or do you not know that as many of us as were baptized into Christ Jesus were baptized into His death? Therefore we were buried with Him through baptism into death, that just as Christ was raised from the dead by the glory of the Father, even so we also should walk in newness of life. For if we have been united together in the likeness of His death, certainly we also shall be in the likeness of His resurrection (Romans 6:2–5).

Water baptism is a public testimony that we have died to sin and self and live for God.

3. When Christ is the center of our being we are alive to God's will (4:1–2). As the believer comes up out of the water, the resurrection of Jesus from death is symbolized, testifying of our eternal hope of resurrection at the coming of Christ Jesus. So it symbolizes the power and presence of the Holy Spirit to live a new life for the will of God. No longer do the passions of the flesh entice you. You will not participate in the satisfying of baser desires. Your satisfaction is found in the ultimate desire—the desire for God—the hunger for God. Water baptism testifies to your desire and commitment of exclusive loyalty to the will of God.

Conclusion: Water baptism is not an option in the Christian life. It is a necessary part of our testimony. When Christ is central to our being we will have hope, we will die to sin and self, we will be alive to the will of God. Baptism symbolizes this reality of being dead center with Christ. Will you consider participating in this rite of water baptism? Will you publicly testify that you have died to sin and live for Christ?

Administering the Lord's Supper/Communion
By Rev. Todd Kinde

The Lord's Supper is traditionally celebrated after the ministry of the Word. The sermon is the audible expression of the gospel, while the Lord's Supper is the visible expression of the gospel. Conclude the Word portion of the worship service with a song of response that will apply the truths of the sermon to the hearts of the people and that will move attention to the table of the Lord.

Sample Order of Service for Observance of the Lord's Supper/Communion

The Apostles' Creed	*Distribution of Elements*
Passing of the Peace	*Prayers of the People*
Instructions	*Benevolent Offering*
Words of Institution	*Benediction*
Great Prayer of Thanksgiving	

Sample Detailed Lord's Supper/ Communion Service

The Apostles' Creed: *The creed is often used as a response to the sermon when communion is to be celebrated. The creed reaffirms the essence of the Christian faith in the hearts of the people. Some congregations may choose to omit "He descended into hell" for theological reasons. The pastor addresses everyone present at the service.*

Minister: Christians, what do you believe?

Congregation: We believe in God, the Father Almighty, Maker of heaven and earth. We believe in Jesus Christ, His only Son, our Lord: who was conceived by the Holy Spirit, and born of the virgin Mary. He suffered under Pontius Pilate, was crucified, died, and was buried. He descended into hell; the third day He rose again from the dead; He ascended to heaven and is seated at the right hand of God the Father Almighty. From there He will come to judge the living and the dead. We believe in the Holy Spirit, the holy catholic/Christian church, the communion of saints, the forgiveness of sins, the resurrection of the body, and the life everlasting. Amen.

Passing of the Peace: *When Jesus appeared to His disciples after His resurrection He most frequently greeted them saying, "Peace be with you." Communion is a good time to express to one another a prayer that asks for the blessing of peace from Jesus. It may be a time to forgive one another and restore relationships.*

The pastor extends his arms and hands toward the people and says,

The peace of Christ be with you all!

The people respond,

And also with you!

The people then turn to one another and repeat the phrase to other individuals while perhaps shaking hands or embracing. Do not rush the expression; allow time for people to move about the room.

The communion stewards may take their positions at this time.

Instructions: *The pastor should instruct the people as to the procedures of the Lord's Supper. If all are to partake together, then indicate that each should hold their portion until all have been served. This is an appropriate time to instruct the people as to the seriousness of the ordinance/sacrament and that it should not be entered into lightly. Inform them that the table is for believers who are in right relation with one another. If your fellowship observes a closed communion, that is, only for those who are members of your local church or denomination, indicate so.*

Words of Institution: *The pastor will take the loaf of bread from the communion table and break it saying,*

The Lord Jesus on the same night in which He was betrayed took bread; and when He had given thanks, He broke it and said, "Take, eat; this is My body which is broken for you; do this in remembrance of Me" (1 Corinthians 11:23–24).

The pastor will take the cup from the communion table and lift it, saying,

In the same manner He also took the cup after supper, saying, "This cup is the new covenant in My blood. This do, as often as you drink it, in remembrance of Me." For as often as you eat this bread and drink this cup, you proclaim the Lord's death till He comes (1 Corinthians 11:25–26).

Great Prayer of Thanksgiving: Father, we come to this table as your guests, resting only in the worthiness of your Son. As we look upon the emblems of our Savior's death may we remember why He died—to cleanse and to heal; to satisfy your righteousness and justice. We remember His eternal love and boundless grace. May we receive the assurance of forgiveness, eternal life, and the hope of glory. As the bread and cup nourish our body, so may your indwelling Holy Spirit strengthen our soul, until the day of Christ's appearing when we will hunger and thirst no more, and sit with Him at His heavenly table. Amen.

The prayer may conclude with all the people praying aloud the Lord's Prayer. This may be spoken or sung.

Our Father in heaven,
Hallowed be Your name.
Your kingdom come.
Your will be done
On earth as it is in heaven.
Give us this day our daily bread.
And forgive us our debts,

As we forgive our debtors.
And do not lead us into temptation,
But deliver us from the evil one.
For Yours is the kingdom and the power and the glory for-
ever. Amen (Matthew 6:9–13).

Distribution of the Elements: *The distribution of the
elements may be done in silence, with musical back-
ground, or with congregational singing.*

*The pastor gives to the communion stewards the trays/
baskets containing the bread. Real pieces of a whole
grain bread add to the symbolism of one body from one
loaf. When the communion stewards have distributed
the bread to all the people who are partaking they will
return the trays/baskets to the pastor at the table. The
pastor then serves the communion stewards. The pastor
asks the people to stand together and raises his own portion, saying to the people,*

The body of our Lord Jesus Christ, which is given for us.
Let us eat together.

*The pastor gives to the communion stewards the trays
containing the cup. When the communion stewards
have distributed the cup to all the people who are partaking they will return the trays to the pastor at the table. The pastor then serves the communion stewards.
The pastor asks the people to stand together and raises
his own portion, saying to the people,*

The blood of our Lord Jesus Christ through which we have
the forgiveness of sins. Let us drink together.

Prayers of the People: *A time of prayer follows the Lord's Supper. The people of the congregation may do these prayers as the pastor introduces specific topics or people may come to the table area for silent prayer or to pray with another person. Having people gifted in intercessory prayer available to pray with those coming may also be helpful. The pastor may, however, choose a pastoral prayer for the congregation at this time.*

Benevolent Offering: *A benevolent offering may be collected for the needy of the local church or for a special project within your fellowship of churches or denomination.*

Benediction: *The pastor will ask the people to stand for the blessing. The benediction may be a Scripture verse that culminates the theme of the sermon or of the Lord's Supper.*

The grace of the Lord Jesus Christ, and the love of God, and the communion of the Holy Spirit be with you all. Amen (2 Corinthians 13:14).

Agape Meal/
Communion Service
By Todd Kinde

The Love Feast or Agape meal is mentioned in the New Testament as a gathering of the local church to celebrate the Lord's Supper. This meal was a common meal shared together. The bread and the cup form the main features of this simple meal. It is a wonderful expression of unity within the fellowship of believers. An evening setting in a fellowship hall would work well for the Agape meal. Families can sit together at tables throughout the service.

The meal should be rather simple to keep the focus on the holy ordinance/sacrament of the Lord's Supper. Place the food on the table before the service begins to eliminate movement during the service itself. For example, fixings can be placed on the table to make sandwiches along with chips or pretzels. In the fall and winter seasons soup may also be part of this meal. The congregation may enjoy participating by bringing various desserts to share, which could be placed on a buffet table.

Place large loaves of bread on the center of each table. Also place a candle at the center of each table to represent Christ who is the Light of the world. A small cup of wine or grape juice should be pre-poured and placed at each table setting. You may desire to have separate cups for the main beverage of the meal.

Either in the center of the room among the tables or at the front of the room place a small table where a symbolic communion bread and cup can be placed. Be sure the table is tall enough for the people to see. The pastor will break this bread and lift this cup during the actual words of institution.

The length of this service and meal is about 90 minutes.

Sample Order of Service for an Agape Meal and Communion

Prelude

Words of Welcome

Songs of Gathering

Invocation

Lighting the Christ Candle

Scripture Reading

Song of Response

Scripture Meditation

Passing of the Peace

Great Prayer of Thanksgiving

Breaking of the Bread

Drinking of the Cup

Song of Thanksgiving

Agape Meal

Benediction

Sample Detailed Agape Meal and Communion Service

Prelude: *The music should be simple and inviting, played quietly as people arrive.*

Words of Welcome: *Some words greeting the people as they arrive and gather at the tables may be spoken. These words should have a sense of warmth and hospitality, like a family gathering.*

Songs of Gathering: *Select songs that reflect the nature of your worshiping community but keep them focused on the reason for gathering—the Lord's Supper. Two or three songs should be adequate. Instrumental accompaniment to the singing may be an acoustic guitar, digital keyboard or piano. Singing may also be done a* cappella *very effectively in this intimate setting.*

Invocation: Savior God we have gathered together in Your name. Be pleased to honor this gathering with Your blessed presence. May our communion with You be warm. May our fellowship with one another be sweet. Amen.

Lighting the Christ Candle: "Then Jesus spoke to them again, saying, 'I am the light of the world. He who follows Me shall not walk in darkness, but have the light of life'" (John 8:12).

Let us light the Christ Candle at our tables.

One member at each table may light the Christ Candle. Be sure matches are at each table.

Scripture Reading: *Select a passage of Scripture that focuses on the work of Christ for our salvation and/or the fellowship we share because of His completed work for us. Seasonal passages work well such as at Advent, Christmas, Lent, Easter, Pentecost and so on. This Scripture reading may be used as the basis for the meditation to follow.*

Song of Response: *Select a song that reflects upon the themes of the Scripture reading. A simple song of* *thanks and praise will also work well in response to the reading of the Word.*

Scripture Meditation: *The meditation should be brief—perhaps ten minutes in length.*

Passing of the Peace: *When Jesus appeared to His disciples after His resurrection He most frequently greeted them saying, "Peace be with you." The Agape meal is good time to express to one another a prayer that asks for the blessing of peace from Jesus. It may be a time to forgive one another and restore relationships.*

The pastor extends his arms and hands toward the people and says,

The peace of Christ be with you all!

The people respond,

And also with you!

The people then turn to one another and repeat the phrase to individuals perhaps shaking hands or embracing. Do not rush the expression; allow time for people to move about the room.

Great Prayer of Thanksgiving: *When the people appear to have completed the passing of the peace to one another the pastor then prays over the elements of the Lord's Table.*

Father, we come to this table as Your guests resting only in the worthiness of Your Son. As we look upon the emblems of our Savior's death may we remember why He died—to cleanse and to heal; to satisfy your righteousness and justice. We remember His eternal love and boundless grace. May we receive the assurance of forgiveness, eternal life, and the hope of glory. As the bread and cup nourish our body, so may Your indwelling Holy Spirit strengthen our soul, until the day of Christ's appearing when we will hunger and thirst no more, and sit with Him at His heavenly table. Amen.

Breaking of the Bread: *The pastor will take a loaf of bread from the small table in the center or front of the room and break it, saying,*

The Lord Jesus on the same night in which He was betrayed took bread; and when He had given thanks, He broke it and said, "Take, eat; this is My body which is broken for you; do this in remembrance of Me" (1 Corinthians 11:23–24).

A member from each table then breaks or slices a piece of bread from the loaf at each table, taking a smaller piece from it for himself and then passing the larger piece to the others at that table. When all have been served the pastor may raise his portion and say,

The body of our Lord Jesus Christ, which is given for us. Let us eat together.

Drinking of the Cup: *The pastor will take the cup from the small table in the center or front of the room and lift it, saying,*

In the same manner He also took the cup after supper, saying, "This cup is the new covenant in My blood. This do, as often as you drink it, in remembrance of Me." For as often as you eat this bread and drink this cup, you proclaim the Lord's death till He comes (1 Corinthians 11:25–26).

Each member at the tables may take the cup that is at their place setting. The pastor will say,

The blood of our Lord Jesus Christ through which we have the forgiveness of sins. Let us drink together.

Song of Thanksgiving: *This song should be a joyful expression of gratitude to God for redemption.*

Agape Meal: *Give instructions as to the eating of the meal. Keep the meal simple and try to have all the needed elements for the meal already on the tables. Use the loaf that was part of the communion service as a main part of the meal. You may want to place the bread on a breadboard and provide a bread knife. When the people are finished eating the main meal they may go to the dessert table that has been filled with desserts brought by the people.*

Benediction: *The pastor will address the people and perhaps share some family items of concern to the fellowship. The pastor will then conclude the Agape meal with a blessing.*

May you walk in the light as He is in the light. May you have fellowship with one another, for the blood of Jesus Christ His Son cleanses us from all sin (adapted from 1 John 1:7).

Communion Sermon
By Rev. Richard Sharpe

Remember the Sacrifice

Scripture: 1 Corinthians 11:23–32

Introduction: The Corinthian church was a troubled church with many problems. We say that all churches have problems because they have people in them. The people in this particular church of Corinth were people who had no problem putting up with sin among other church members. They had no reservations against treating some people better than others. They had no qualms about withholding their food from those who were less fortunate. At the beginning of the church there was a fellowship dinner called a "love feast," which was followed by communion. Some call this the Agape meal and still practice it in modern churches. Everyone was to bring something to this feast and share what they brought with everyone who attended, much like our modern pot-luck dinners. Imagine someone withholding their pot-luck stew from certain members of this congregation; that's what was happening! Paul strongly opposed this behavior. In his letter, he warned them that they were not honoring the memory of Christ's death for their sins. In fact, he told them that they were sinning at the communion table. He wanted it to stop. Listen to this passage as we unpack it.

1. Proper elements for the Lord's Supper (vv. 23–26).

> For I received from the Lord that which I also delivered to you: that the Lord Jesus on the same night in which He was betrayed took bread; and when He had given thanks, He broke it and said, "Take, eat;

this is My body which is broken for you; do this in remembrance of Me." In the same manner He also took the cup after supper, saying, "This cup is the new covenant in My blood. This do, as often as you drink it, in remembrance of Me." For as often as you eat this bread and drink this cup, you proclaim the Lord's death till He comes.

Paul received instructions from Christ regarding the supper. Paul was an apostle who accepted Christ after His crucifixion. He was one who used to persecute the church. He was saved in a miraculous manner. Paul went away for three years to be instructed by Christ; one of the things he was instructed in was this supper. So he shared what he had learned with authority to the Corinthian church. They were instructed in the proper way to celebrate the Lord's death.

A. *The bread.* The bread was to represent the body of Christ that died on the Cross for our sins. He suffered many abuses on his way to the Cross. His body was in rough shape on the Cross. He suffered on the Cross. He gave His all for us.

B. *The cup.* The cup was to represent the blood of Christ that He shed on the Cross for our sins. The Bible says that without the shedding of blood there is no forgiveness of sin (Hebrews 9:22). Christ had to shed His blood for us. The animal sacrifices in the Old Testament looked forward to the time when Christ would shed His blood for the sins of the world. This sacrifice was the final one needed to save the world. His blood was enough for all those who accept Him as their personal Savior. Paul tells us that celebrating with these elements reminds the people of the church of Christ's sacrifice. We so often and so easily forget; we often complain about small sacrifices we must make, ignoring the incredible sacrifice of Jesus' body and blood!

2. **Proper attitude for the Lord's Supper** (vv. 27–29).

> Therefore whoever eats this bread or drinks this cup of the Lord in an unworthy manner will be guilty of the body and blood of the Lord. But let a man examine himself, and so let him eat of the bread and drink of the cup. For he who eats and drinks in an unworthy manner eats and drinks judgment to himself, not discerning the Lord's body.

There are two ways someone could take the Lord's Supper. Paul makes this clear to the members of this church. He makes it plain to us as well. What makes the difference?

A. *Those who examine themselves before taking the supper.* The ones who examine themselves before they partake of the supper are the ones who are taking it in a worthy manner. For what are they examining themselves? For sin; sin keeps us from a right relationship with the Lord. When we examine ourselves, we are to confess it. God has promised to forgive us and restore us to a proper fellowship with Him (1 John 1:9).

B. *Those who are judged for not examining themselves.* This group is made up of individuals in the church who choose to come to church flippantly, not taking seriously sin that may be plaguing their lives. They might be people who have accepted Christ as their Savior but are living an uncommitted life. They are those that we sometimes call "Sunday Christians;" those outside the church call these people "hypocrites." This group is known to the pastor as individuals who sit, soak, and sour in the pews. They are usually the ones who find fault in everything in the church. They are those who normally are not involved in daily Bible reading. There are many things that separate them from God. This type of person should reflect and repent before taking the Lord's Supper, for the Lord will not tolerate this behavior; there are consequences:

> For this reason many are weak and sick among you, and many sleep. For if we would judge ourselves, we would not be judged. But when we are judged, we are chastened by the Lord, that we may not be condemned with the world (vv. 30–32).

a. Many become weak and sickly. This type of judgment is called "chastening." Those individuals who have accepted Christ as their Savior, but are not living for the Lord, will be judged by the Lord. If any of you is living a life of sin, but is not being chastened or disciplined, check yourself to be sure you are a true believer. The Bible says, "For whom the Lord loves He chastens, and scourges every son whom He receives" (Hebrews 12:6). We see many Christians who are in this condition. I once visited a hospital room where a woman was having a health issue. She said to me privately that she knew she was having this problem because she was involved in an affair. She confessed the sin to the Lord and she was healed. Before you involve yourself in the remembrance of Christ's sacrifice, repent, be restored, and renewed.

b. Many die. This judgment is terminal. The Bible uses the term "sleep" when it talks about a Christian's death. Here we find that some Christians die prematurely because of sin in their lives. I had a teenager in one of my churches who had a problem with drinking. He came to the parsonage on a regularly basis wondering what to do with this problem. I gave him some suggestions, which he never followed. He "needed" to be with his friends. One night the friends challenged him to drink a bottle of whiskey after he had consumed a lot of beer. He died of the combination. He knew what needed to be done, but he didn't want to give up his friends. Friends, don't let it go this far. Cut sin off at its roots, for Scripture tells us, ". . . when desire has conceived, it gives birth to sin; and sin, when it is full-grown, brings forth death" (James 1:15).

Conclusion: The Corinthian church had some real problems. The church today has many of the same problems. There are Christians who come to the Lord's table without examining their lives. They are challenging God's Word; they will lose. God is going to deal with His children. If you are here today and have not been examining your life for sin, I would challenge you today to examine your relationship with the Lord. Are you in fellowship with Him? Are you keeping short accounts with Him? If there is sin in your life, are you willing to confess it, turn from it, and follow the Lord more closely? Only you can make that decision. The Lord's Supper can be an experience of worship and worthiness, a time of repentance and remembrance, or it can be a time of disobedience which will result in God's ultimate discipline. Let's spend some time in prayer and self-examination before we partake in the Lord's Supper.

Worship

Worship Design Worksheet
By Jerry Carraway

Theme _____ Date _____

Preacher _____ Worship Leader _____

Pre-Service:
- ❑ Announcements
- ❑ Recorded Music
- ❑ Live Music

Praise and Worship:

- ❑ _____
- ❑ _____
- ❑ _____
- ❑ _____

- ❑ _____
- ❑ _____
- ❑ _____
- ❑ _____

- ❑ Choir: _____
- ❑ Solo or other musical offering: _____
- ❑ Prayers: _____

The Spoken Word:
- ❑ Scripture(s): _____ Reader: _____
- ❑ Message Title: _____

Response:
- ❑ Closing Hymn/Hymn of Response: _____
- ❑ Offering: _____
- ❑ Benediction: _____

Other Elements:

- ❑ Drama: _____
- ❑ Video: _____
- ❑ Testimonies: _____
- ❑ Children's Message: _____
- ❑ Baptism: _____
- ❑ Prayer-time: _____
- ❑ Other: _____

Invocations

The invocation is a short, formal prayer usually prayed near the beginning of a worship service, beseeching God's mercy and His presence. The invocation may be specific to the event (wedding, funeral, etc.) or may be general as the following suggestions.

Father, O Maker of heaven and earth, as we gather in Your glorious presence, make us worthy to stand before You though the sacrifice of Your Son, Jesus Christ, in whose name we pray, Amen.

Search us, O God, and know our hearts; try us, and know our anxieties; and see if there is any wicked way in us, and lead us in the way everlasting, Amen (from Psalm 139:23–24).

Lord, we pray with the psalmist, "As the deer pants for the water brooks, so pants our souls for You, O God. Our souls thirsts for God, for the living God . . ." (adapted from Psalm 42:1–2). So now in Your mercy grant us Your grace and guidance, in Jesus' name, Amen.

Who can understand his errors? Cleanse us from secret faults. Keep back Your servants also from presumptuous sins; let them not have dominion over us. Then we shall be blameless, and we shall be innocent of great transgression. Let the words of our mouths and the meditation of our hearts be acceptable in Your sight, O Lord, our strength and our Redeemer, Amen (from Psalm 19:12–14).

Dear Lord, Abraham could not number the stars, but You know them all by name; how much more You know us, O Lord. You clothe the fields in splendor, and how much more You have provided for us, O Lord. And now we trust that You will bless us today as we gather in Your name, Amen.

Lord, as the psalmist said, "I was glad when they said to me, 'Let us go into the house of the Lord'" (Psalm 122:1), let us be glad before You, in Your Spirit this day, Amen.

God of Abraham, Isaac, and Jacob, You are always faithful to Your covenant and to Your people. Forgive our sin and renew our hearts before You today, Amen.

Holy God who knows us by name, we come to You as Moses did, saying, "If Your Presence does not go with us, do not bring us up from here" (Exodus 33:15). For without Your Presence, our worship and our very existence are in vain. Be always with us, Amen.

Who can fathom Your greatness, O God, for Your glory fills the earth! Yet not even a sparrow falls to the ground apart from Your hand. So, Lord, in Your glory and in Your grace, guide us in Your Holy Spirit, in Jesus' name, Amen.

Offertory Prayers

Lord, as we give our tithes and offerings today, we recognize that we are merely stewards of Your resources. We trust that You will bless these gifts for Your kingdom's sake. In Jesus' name, Amen.

O Father in heaven, You have told us that we will reap what we sow. This is true not only in our character, but in our conduct. We want to trust You today with our tithes and offerings, knowing that You are trustworthy to use them for Your kingdom and to continue in Your provision for us. For Your Word says, "He who sows sparingly will also reap sparingly, and he who sows bountifully will also reap bountifully. So let each one give as he purposes in his heart, not grudgingly or of necessity; for God loves a cheerful giver" (2 Corinthians 9:6–7). Help us to be cheerful givers today, in Jesus' name, Amen.

Lord of heaven and earth, in perspective of Your worthiness, we ask You to use our offerings this day for the preaching of Your Word, for the provision of Your witnesses, and for the proclamation of Your works throughout the earth. Amen.

Father, as Your Son was in the temple, He saw the rich offering large amounts of money, but singled out a poor woman who gave but a few cents, saying, "Assuredly, I say to You that this poor widow has put in more than all those who have given to the treasury; for they all put in out of their abundance, but she out of her poverty put in all that she had, her whole livelihood" (Mark 12:43–44). Whether rich or poor, help us to give sacrificially. Bless our tithes and offerings now, in Jesus' name, Amen.

God, You water the fields and feed all the animals of the earth. Your provision is abundant and evident in Your world and in our lives. We ask now that You grant us a generous spirit and a trusting heart, that You might be Lord of these resources that we now give back to You, in Jesus' name, Amen.

O Lord our Maker and Our God, we trust You today to bless our tithes and offerings to advance Your kingdom. We also trust You to continue in Your faithful provision to us, for You said, " 'Bring all the tithes into the storehouse, that there may be food in My house, and try Me now in this,' says the Lord of hosts, 'If I will not open for You the windows of heaven and pour out for You such blessing that there will not be room enough to receive it'" (Malachi 3:10)

Lord, as we gather in Your presence, in this house of worship and prayer, we cannot help but recognize Your goodness to us. Like the psalmist, each day we ". . . taste and see that the Lord is good" (Psalm 34:8). In view of Your mercy and Your provision, especially the ultimate sacrifice of Jesus Christ on the cross of Calvary, we willingly give to You our tithes and offerings. We ask that You bless it for Your sake and for ours, in Jesus' name we pray, Amen.

Benedictions

General: Dismiss us now, O Lord, in Your name. Send us forth in Your strength. Keep us in Your care. For Thine is the kingdom, the power, and the glory forever. Amen.

Keep us safe through this day, O Lord. Keep us safe through this week until we again return to praise Your name in the assembly of the saints. Amen.

Dismiss us with Your love, O Lord. Bless and keep us, our Father, and may God be with us till we meet again.

May the great God of Heaven and Jesus Christ our Lord overwhelm our minds, overcome our weaknesses, and overhear our praise throughout this day and week, to His glory. Amen.

And now, Heavenly Father, may we leave this place to give light to those who sit in darkness and in the shadow of death, and to guide their feet in the way of peace. Amen.

Dismiss us from this place with Your blessing, matchless and mighty and powerful, in the name of Jesus we pray. Amen.

The grace of the Lord Jesus Christ, and the love of God, and the communion of the Holy Spirit be with you all. Amen.

O God, grant to us now glimpses of Your beauty, and make us worthy at length to behold it unveiled for evermore; through Jesus Christ our Lord. Amen.

Now may the Lord use us this week to extend and strengthen His kingdom for Christ and His glory, in Jesus' name, Amen.

Dismiss us, Father, with a victorious heart. Send us on our way as more than conquerors. Give us this week a spirit of triumph. In Jesus' name, Amen.

As we leave from this place, O Lord, may each of us say with the ancient prophet: Here am I, send me. Draw us to be worshipers, and send us to be workers this week. We pray in Jesus' name. Amen.

Thank You, Lord, for the songs that have gone out. Thank You for the supplications that have gone up. Thank You for the sermon that has gone forth. Now, O Lord, let us leave to serve until we meet again hence, or in that better world. Amen.

From Scripture: "The LORD bless you and keep you; the LORD make His face shine upon you, and be gracious to you; the LORD lift up His countenance upon you, and give you peace" (Numbers 6:24–26).

"Let the words of our mouths and the meditation of our hearts be acceptable in Your sight, O Lord, our strength and our Redeemer" (adapted from Psalm 19:14).

May God's goodness and mercy follow you every day and hour this week, and may we dwell in the house of the Lord forever. Amen (from Psalm 23).

"Help us, O God of our salvation, for the glory of Your name; and deliver us, and provide atonement for our sins, for Your name's sake" (Psalm 79:9).

"May the glory of the Lord endure forever; may the LORD rejoice in His works" (Psalm 104:31).

"Now may the God of patience and comfort grant you to be like-minded toward one another, according to Christ Jesus, that you may with one mind and one mouth glorify the God and Father of our Lord Jesus Christ" (Romans 15:5–6).

"The grace of the Lord Jesus Christ, and the love of God, and the communion of the Holy Spirit be with you all. Amen" (2 Corinthians 13:14).

"Now to the King eternal, immortal, invisible, to God who alone is wise, be honor and glory forever and ever. Amen" (1 Timothy 1:17).

"To Him who is the blessed and only Potentate, the King of kings and Lord of lords, who alone has immortality, dwelling in unapproachable light, whom no man has seen or can see—to Him be honor and everlasting power. Amen" (1 Timothy 6:15–16).

"Grace, mercy, and peace from God the Father and Christ Jesus our Lord" (2 Timothy 1:2).

"Now may the God of peace who brought up our Lord Jesus from the dead, that great Shepherd of the sheep, through the blood of the everlasting covenant, make you complete in every good work to do His will, working in you what is well pleasing in His sight, through Jesus Christ, to whom be glory forever and ever. Amen" (Hebrews 13:20–21).

". . . To Him be the glory both now and forever. Amen" (2 Peter 3:18).

"Now to Him who is able to keep you from stumbling, and to present you faultless before the presence of His glory with exceeding joy, to God our Savior, Who alone is wise, be glory and majesty, dominion and power, both now and forever. Amen" (Jude 24–25).

"To Him who loved us and washed us from our sins in His own blood, and has made us kings and priests to His God and Father, to Him be glory and dominion forever and ever. Amen" (Revelation 1:5, 6).

Church Year Calendar

This calendar is an outline of major events each year concerning the church. Some of the more prominent liturgical dates will be briefly explained. Since the calendar shifts each year, specific dates will not be given, but may be determined based on the dates for Christmas and Easter on any given calendar year.

Epiphany: Our English word "epiphany" comes from a Greek word meaning "manifestation" or "showing." It falls every year on January 6th. It is often called "Twelfth Day," "Three Kings Day," or "Little Christmas." This date commemorates the visit of the wise men to Bethlehem; Eastern Churches celebrate the baptism of Jesus on this date, some, the Miracle at Cana. The eve of Epiphany is often called "Twelfth Night." Epiphany is often celebrated on the Sunday between January 2nd and 8th.

The Feast of the Lord's Baptism: In Western churches, the Sunday following Epiphany celebrates the end of the Christmas season with the Feast of the Lord's Baptism.

Sanctity of Human Life Sunday: This event is a designated time for ministers and congregations to unite and focus on the value and sanctity of human life. Traditionally, this day falls on the Sunday nearest to the anniversary of the Supreme Court's *Roe* v. *Wade* decision of January 22, 1973. Many denominations have chosen the third Sunday of January to recognize this day. However, this Sunday can conflict with the observance of Martin Luther King Jr.'s Birthday, which causes competition between two most important civil rights events. Many congregations thus observe a

Sanctity of Human Life Week, which includes both the third and fourth Sundays of January.

Ash Wednesday: Ash Wednesday is the first day of Lent. It falls on the Wednesday which is 40 days before Easter. This day marks the start of the season of discipline which is meant to prepare worshipers for Easter. The 40 days are reminiscent of Jesus' 40-day fast in the wilderness after His baptism.

Holy Week: Often called "Passion Week," Holy week is the week preceding Easter which celebrates several of the final events in the life of Christ:

> **Palm Sunday:** Palm Sunday is the Sunday before Easter. This date marks the beginning of Holy Week. Palm Sunday is based around the triumphal entry of Jesus into Jerusalem, when crowds spread palms and clothing in front of Jesus. Palm Sunday turns attention from the days of discipline which preceded to a looking ahead to the suffering and death of Jesus followed by His resurrection.

> **Spy Wednesday:** In some traditions, this day recognizes the betrayal of Jesus by Judas Iscariot who accepts a bribe to turn Jesus over to the Jewish leaders.

> **Maundy Thursday:** Often called Holy Thursday, Maundy Thursday recalls the Last Supper in which Jesus instituted a New Covenant, after which He was arrested in the Garden of Gethsemane. On Maundy Thursday, many Protestant churches hold Communion, while Catholics hold a special Mass.

Good Friday: This date observes the crucifixion and death of Jesus Christ on the Cross. Many churches hold mourning services; some services last from noon until three o'clock, symbolizing the final three hours of darkness when Jesus suffered and finally died on the Cross. Traditionally, Christians fast or eat little food on Good Friday.

Holy Saturday: Roman Catholic and Eastern Orthodox churches often hold candlelight vigil services starting at nightfall on this day. These services often include the baptism of new members. The climax of this event occurs when each person blows out his or her candle. The priest or minister then lights one candle, representing the resurrected Christ. The flame is then passed from person to person, representing Jesus as the light of the world. In Eastern Orthodox churches, this service is timed so that the priest or minister lights his candle at midnight exactly. After each candle has been lit, the ceremony then becomes an Easter celebration.

Easter Sunday: Easter is celebrated on the first Sunday after the first full moon after the Vernal Equinox. It is much easier to consult any secular calendar to find the specific date. Easter Sunday celebrates the resurrection of Jesus Christ from the dead, and His appearance to many witnesses. Often sunrise services are held which symbolize the newly risen Christ.

National Day of Prayer: A joint resolution by Congress in 1952, signed by President Truman, initiated a yearly, national day of prayer. In 1988, this law was amended by President Reagan, permanently establishing the first Thursday of every May as the National Day of Prayer. Each year the president signs a proclamation which encourages all Americans to have a special time of prayer on this day.

Mother's Day: This holiday honors mothers, and always falls on the second Sunday in May.

Ascension Day: This day falls 40 days after Easter and is always on a Thursday. It is quite possibly the earliest observed holiday in Christianity, recognizing Christ's Ascension into the heavens after His Resurrection. Churches sometimes have special services this day, or will celebrate this event the Sunday after it.

Father's Day: This holiday honors fathers, and always falls on the third Sunday in June.

Pentecost: Pentecost is recognized the Sunday, 50 days after Easter, recalling when the apostles gathered in the Upper Room and the Holy Spirit descended on the people, who were then preached to by Peter and converted to become the first group of New Testament believers.

Trinity Sunday: Because it was after Pentecost that the doctrine of the Trinity began to spread throughout the world, this Sunday is aptly named "Trinity Sunday." Teaching on this Sunday revolves around the theological doctrine of the Trinity.

Transfiguration Day: Recognized on August 6th, this event commemorates the transfiguration on Mt. Tabor when Jesus' physical appearance became radiant and Moses and Elijah appeared with Him and the Father's voice was audibly heard.

Reformation Day: Recognized on the last Sunday in October, Reformation Day commemorates Martin Luther's posting of his *Ninety-Five Theses* on the door of the Castle Church in Wittenberg, which triggered the movement known as the Protestant Reformation.

All Hallow's Eve: This date is always October 31st. All Hallow's Eve in some traditions includes prayer and celebration involving the entire family in preparation for All Saints Day.

All Saints Day: Commemorating and honoring saints, known and unknown, All Saints Day falls on November 1st. It is a "Holy Day of Obligation" in the Roman Catholic Church, in which saints have special status. Saints, generally, are people who have led unusual lives of piety, holiness, and devotion to God.

All Souls Day: Held November 2nd, All Souls Day originates from a Roman Catholic tradition of intercessory prayers for the dead.

International Day of Prayer for the Persecuted Church: The International Day of Prayer for the Persecuted Church usually falls on the second or third Sunday of November. It is an international day of involvement of Christians in intercession for the worldwide persecuted church. The primary focus is to involve all Christians in intercession for persecuted communities of believers, and secondarily it is to heighten awareness and pro-activity concerning this issue.

Thanksgiving Day: This day is celebrated the fourth Thursday of November each year to commemorate God's provision in American history: After arriving in Massachusetts in late November, 1620, Protestant Pilgrims attempted to find a landing place. After landing, they quickly began to build shelter after corporate prayer. The pilgrims were not prepared for a harsh winter in New England and almost half of them died before spring. With the help of Indians and through prayer, the Pilgrims reaped an incredible harvest the following summer. The Pilgrims then instituted a three-day feast to thank God for His provision. Although this was not the first Thanksgiving service held in America, it was the first Thanksgiving festival.

Advent: Advent begins the Christian church year, but is held at the end of the calendar year. It begins on the Sunday nearest St. Andrew's Day (which is held November 30th), and continues until Christmas Eve (December 24th). The term "Advent" comes from the Latin word *adventus,* which means coming or arrival. Advent is the season in which many Christians prepare for the celebration of the birth of Jesus Christ on Christmas Day. Many Christians hang an Advent wreath in their homes during this season. On these wreaths, made of holly branches or evergreen, four candles are placed, one for each Sunday of Advent. Often, three of the candles are dark purple, and the fourth is pink or light purple; this candle is not lit until the third Sunday on which is celebrated the second half of Advent. Often, a large red candle is added to the wreath on Christmas day symbolizing the birth of Jesus Christ. Church services often include a different family each week to represent the church-wide family involvement in the Sundays of Advent.

First Sunday of Advent: On the first Sunday, a family lights one candle and joins in prayer. In church services, the wreath is often excluded and candles are set up solitarily. They repeat this ceremony on each Sunday of Advent, lighting one additional candle each service. Traditional texts read are: Matthew 24:37–44; Mark 13:33–37; Luke 21:25–28, 34–36.

Second Sunday of Advent: The second Sunday of Advent involves a family lighting a second candle and joining in a prayer. Traditional texts are: Matthew 3:1–12; Mark 1:1–8; Luke 3:1–6.

Third Sunday of Advent: The third Sunday of Advent, like the second, involves a family lighting a second candle and joining in prayer. Traditional texts are: Matthew 11:2–11; John 1:6–8, 19–28; Luke 3:10–18.

Fourth Sunday of Advent: This final Sunday of Advent has the most climactic tone. It anticipates the Nativity of Christ most of all. The family shall light the final candle and join in prayer. Traditional texts are: Matthew 1:18–24; Luke 1:26–38; Luke 1:39–45.

Christmas Day: Christmas celebrates the birth of the Messiah, Jesus Christ, in a manger in Bethlehem. This day is celebrated December 25 each year.

Pastoral Care

Pastoral visitation to hospitals and homes is one of the most important duties of the man of God, and especially of the minister of God. In this he will have the opportunity to provide a healing, helping, guiding, and encouraging presence to those in need. If they are believers, he can remind them of God's care, His presence, and His help in this time of need. If they are yet unsaved, he may gently remind them of God's love and willingness to forgive and to save. People truly need the pastor or minister's love, prayer, friendship, understanding, counsel, and sympathy.

Dr. W. A. Criswell said, "Every opportunity is a golden invitation from the courts of heaven to be a messenger of encouragement and salvation. The very angels must envy our place of service."

Hospital Visitation Checklist
By Dr. Charles A. Thigpen

1. Remember that you are God's representative, God's servant.

2. Talk about the Lord; the visit must be spiritual in nature.

3. Make the visit friendly and casual, not stiff and formal.

4. Depend upon God for guidance, understanding, and direction.

5. Purpose that your visit will be uplifting, expressing Christian joy.

6. Determine to bring cheer, consolation, comfort, encouragement, and hope to the sick.

7. Show love, concern, and deep personal interest, both for the patient and for family or friends present.

8. Leave your card and return later if your visit is at an inappropriate time.

9. Endeavor to meet spiritual needs of the unsaved and to edify the believer.

10. Be sure your hospital visits are brief—no more than five to ten minutes in length.

11. Read or quote a brief passage of Scripture, and always close with prayer.

Home Visitation Checklist
By Dr. Charles A. Thigpen

1. Remember that you are God's representative, God's servant.

2. Talk about the Lord; the visit must be spiritual in nature.

3. Make the visit friendly and casual, not stiff and formal.

4. Depend upon God for guidance, understanding, and direction.

5. Always call ahead to determine a convenient time for your visit.

6. Learn to listen as needs are shared.

7. Seek to win people to Christ, or to build them up if they are believers.

8. Keep in strict confidence any matters shared with you as pastor.

9. Make necessary arrangements for any counseling needs.

10. Keep your visit under one hour—30 to 45 minutes is ideal.

11. Be very approachable; try to understand the needs and concerns of the person or persons.

12. Read a passage from the Bible and have prayer to close.

Traditional Verses to Share with the Sick or Dying

By Dr. Charles A. Thigpen

Scripture to Share with Believers Who Are Sick

Psalm 8:1–9: O LORD, our Lord, how excellent is Your name in all the earth, who have set Your glory above the heavens! Out of the mouth of babes and nursing infants You have ordained strength, because of Your enemies, that You may silence the enemy and the avenger. When I consider Your heavens, the work of Your fingers, the moon and the stars, which You have ordained, what is man that You are mindful of him, and the son of man that You visit him? For You have made him a little lower than the angels, and You have crowned him with glory and honor. You have made him to have dominion over the works of Your hands; You have put all things under his feet, all sheep and oxen—even the beasts of the field, the birds of the air, and the fish of the sea that pass through the paths of the seas. O LORD, our Lord, how excellent is Your name in all the earth!

Psalm 23:1–6: The LORD is my shepherd; I shall not want. He makes me to lie down in green pastures; He leads me beside the still waters. He restores my soul; He leads me in the paths of righteousness for His name's sake. Yea, though I walk through the valley of the shadow of death, I will fear no evil; for You are with me; Your rod and Your staff, they comfort me. You prepare a table before me in the presence of my enemies; You anoint my head with oil; my cup runs over. Surely goodness and mercy shall follow me all the days of my life; and I will dwell in the house of the LORD forever.

Psalm 46:1–7: God is our refuge and strength, a very present help in trouble. Therefore we will not fear, even though the earth be removed, and though the mountains be carried into the midst of the sea; though its waters roar and be troubled, though the mountains shake with its swelling. Selah. There is a river whose streams shall make glad the city of God, the holy place of the tabernacle of the Most High. God is in the midst of her, she shall not be moved; God shall help her, just at the break of dawn. The nations raged, the kingdoms were moved; He uttered His voice, the earth melted. The LORD of hosts is with us; the God of Jacob is our refuge.

Psalm 96:1–4: Oh, sing to the LORD a new song! Sing to the LORD, all the earth. Sing to the LORD, bless His name; proclaim the good news of His salvation from day to day. Declare His glory among the nations, His wonders among all peoples. For the LORD is great and greatly to be praised; He is to be feared above all gods.

Psalm 118:1–8: Oh, give thanks to the LORD, for He is good! For His mercy endures forever. Let Israel now say, "His mercy endures forever." Let the house of Aaron now say, "His mercy endures forever." Let those who fear the LORD now say, "His mercy endures forever." I called on the LORD in distress; the LORD answered me and set me in a broad place. The LORD is on my side; I will not fear. What can man do to me? The LORD is for me among those who help me; therefore I shall see my desire on those who hate me. It is better to trust in the LORD than to put confidence in man.

John 14:1–6: "Let not your heart be troubled; you believe in God, believe also in Me. In My Father's house are many mansions; if it were not so, I would have told you. I go to prepare a place for you. And if I go and prepare a place for you, I will come again and receive you to Myself; that where I am, there you may be also. And where I go you know, and the way you know." Thomas said to Him, "Lord, we do not know where You are going, and how can we know the way" Jesus said to him, "I am the way, the truth, and the life. No one comes to the Father except through Me."

John 14:13–18: "And whatever you ask in My name, that I will do, that the Father may be glorified in the Son. If you ask anything in My name, I will do it. If you love Me, keep My commandments. And I will pray the Father, and He will give you another Helper, that He may abide with you forever—the Spirit of truth, whom the world cannot receive, because it neither sees Him nor knows Him; but you know Him, for He dwells with you and will be in you. I will not leave you orphans; I will come to you."

John 15:15–17: No longer do I call you servants, for a servant does not know what his master is doing; but I have called you friends, for all things that I heard from My Father I have made known to you. You did not choose Me, but I chose you and appointed you that you should go and bear fruit, and that your fruit should remain, that whatever you ask the Father in My name He may give you. These things I command you, that you love one another.

Romans 5:1–8: Therefore, having been justified by faith, we have peace with God through our Lord Jesus Christ, through whom also we have access by faith into this grace in which we stand, and rejoice in hope of the glory of God.

And not only that, but we also glory in tribulations, knowing that tribulation produces perseverance; and perseverance, character; and character, hope. Now hope does not disappoint, because the love of God has been poured out in our hearts by the Holy Spirit who was given to us. For when we were still without strength, in due time Christ died for the ungodly. For scarcely for a righteous man will one die; yet perhaps for a good man someone would even dare to die. But God demonstrates His own love toward us, in that while we were still sinners, Christ died for us.

Romans 8:26–27: Likewise the Spirit also helps in our weaknesses. For we do not know what we should pray for as we ought, but the Spirit Himself makes intercession for us with groanings which cannot be uttered. Now He who searches the hearts knows what the mind of the Spirit is, because He makes intercession for the saints according to the will of God.

Romans 8:28–34: And we know that all things work together for good to those who love God, to those who are the called according to His purpose. For whom He foreknew, He also predestined to be conformed to the image of His Son, that He might be the firstborn among many brethren. Moreover whom He predestined, these He also called; whom He called, these He also justified; and whom He justified, these He also glorified. What then shall we say to these things? If God is for us, who can be against us? He who did not spare His own Son, but delivered Him up for us all, how shall He not with Him also freely give us all things? Who shall bring a charge against God's elect? It is God who justifies. Who is he who condemns? It is Christ who died, and furthermore is also risen, who is even at the right hand of God, who also makes intercession for us.

Romans 8:35–39: Who shall separate us from the love of Christ? Shall tribulation, or distress, or persecution, or famine, or nakedness, or peril, or sword? As it is written: "For Your sake we are killed all day long; we are accounted as sheep for the slaughter." Yet in all these things we are more than conquerors through Him who loved us. For I am persuaded that neither death nor life, nor angels nor principalities nor powers, nor things present nor things to come, nor height nor depth, nor any other created thing, shall be able to separate us from the love of God which is in Christ Jesus our Lord.

Hebrews 4:14–16: Seeing then that we have a great High Priest who has passed through the heavens, Jesus the Son of God, let us hold fast our confession. For we do not have a High Priest who cannot sympathize with our weaknesses, but was in all points tempted as we are, yet without sin. Let us therefore come boldly to the throne of grace, that we may obtain mercy and find grace to help in time of need.

James 1:2–6: My brethren, count it all joy when you fall into various trials, knowing that the testing of your faith produces patience. But let patience have its perfect work, that you may be perfect and complete, lacking nothing. If any of you lacks wisdom, let him ask of God, who gives to all liberally and without reproach, and it will be given to him. But let him ask in faith, with no doubting, for he who doubts is like a wave of the sea driven and tossed by the wind.

James 5:14–18: Is anyone among you sick? Let him call for the elders of the church, and let them pray over him, anointing him with oil in the name of the Lord. And the prayer of faith will save the sick, and the Lord will raise him up. And if he has committed sins, he will be forgiven. Confess your trespasses to one another, and pray for one another, that you may be healed. The effective, fervent prayer of a righteous man avails much. Elijah was a man with a nature like ours, and he prayed earnestly that it would not rain; and it did not rain on the land for three years and six months. And he prayed again, and the heaven gave rain, and the earth produced its fruit.

1 John 5:1–5: Whoever believes that Jesus is the Christ is born of God, and everyone who loves Him who begot also loves him who is begotten of Him. By this we know that we love the children of God, when we love God and keep His commandments. For this is the love of God, that we keep His commandments. And His commandments are not burdensome. For whatever is born of God overcomes the world. And this is the victory that has overcome the world—our faith. Who is he who overcomes the world, but he who believes that Jesus is the Son of God?

Scripture to Share with
Unbelievers Who Are Sick

Psalm 32:1–5: Blessed is he whose transgression is forgiven, whose sin is covered. Blessed is the man to whom the LORD does not impute iniquity, and in whose spirit there is no deceit. When I kept silent, my bones grew old through my groaning all the day long. For day and night Your hand was heavy upon me; my vitality was turned into the drought of summer. Selah. I acknowledged my sin to You, and my iniquity I have not hidden. I said, "I will confess my transgressions to the Lord," and You forgave the iniquity of my sin.

Isaiah 55:6–7: Seek the Lord while He may be found, call upon Him while He is near. Let the wicked forsake his way, and the unrighteous man his thoughts; let him return to the LORD, and He will have mercy on him; and to our God, for He will abundantly pardon.

John 3:16–18: "For God so loved the world that He gave His only begotten Son, that whoever believes in Him should not perish but have everlasting life. For God did not send His Son into the world to condemn the world, but that the world through Him might be saved. He who believes in Him is not condemned; but he who does not believe is condemned already, because he has not believed in the name of the only begotten Son of God."

Acts 3:19: Repent therefore and be converted, that your sins may be blotted out, so that times of refreshing may come from the presence of the Lord.

Romans 10:9–13: If you confess with your mouth the Lord Jesus and believe in your heart that God has raised Him from the dead, you will be saved. For with the heart one believes unto righteousness, and with the mouth confession is made unto salvation. For the Scripture says, "Whoever believes on Him will not be put to shame." For there is no distinction between Jew and Greek, for ?the same Lord over all is rich to all who call upon Him. For "whoever calls on the name of the Lord shall be saved."

Ephesians 2:8–10: For by grace you have been saved through faith, and that not of yourselves; it is the gift of God, not of works, lest anyone should boast. For we are His workmanship, created in Christ Jesus for good works, which God prepared beforehand that we should walk in them.

Ephesians 3:14–21: For this reason I bow my knees to the Father of our Lord Jesus Christ, from whom the whole family in heaven and earth is named, that He would grant you, according to the riches of His glory, to be strengthened with might through His Spirit in the inner man, that Christ may dwell in your hearts through faith; that you, being rooted and grounded in love, may be able to comprehend with all the saints what is the width and length and depth and height—to know the love of Christ which passes knowledge; that you may be filled with all the fullness of God. Now to Him who is able to do exceedingly abundantly above all that we ask or think, according to the power that works in us, to Him be glory in the church by Christ Jesus to all generations, forever and ever. Amen.

1 John 5:9–13: If we receive the witness of men, the witness of God is greater; for this is the witness of God which

He has testified of His Son. He who believes in the Son of God has the witness in himself; he who does not believe God has made Him a liar, because he has not believed the testimony that God has given of His Son. And this is the testimony: that God has given us eternal life, and this life is in His Son. He who has the Son has life; he who does not have the Son of God does not have life. These things I have written to you who believe in the name of the Son of God, that you may know that you have eternal life, and that you may continue to believe in the name of the Son of God.

Revelation 3:20: Behold, I stand at the door and knock. If anyone hears My voice and opens the door, I will come in to him and dine with him, and he with Me.

Revelation 22:17: And the Spirit and the bride say, "Come!" And let him who hears say, "Come!" And let him who thirsts come. Whoever desires, let him take the water of life freely.

Scripture to Share with the Dying or Bereaved

Psalm 23:1–6: The LORD is my shepherd; I shall not want. He makes me to lie down in green pastures; He leads me beside the still waters. He restores my soul; He leads me in the paths of righteousness for His name's sake. Yea, though I walk through the valley of the shadow of death, I will fear no evil; for You are with me; Your rod and Your staff, they comfort me. You prepare a table before me in the presence of my enemies; You anoint my head with oil; my cup runs over. Surely goodness and mercy shall follow me all the days of my life; and I will dwell in the house of the LORD forever.

Psalm 91:5–7: You shall not be afraid of the terror by night, nor of the arrow that flies by day, nor of the pestilence that walks in darkness, nor of the destruction that lays waste at noonday. A thousand may fall at your side, and ten thousand at your right hand; but it shall not come near you.

Psalm 116:15: Precious in the sight of the LORD is the death of His saints.

John 14:1–6: "Let not your heart be troubled; you believe in God, believe also in Me. In My Father's house are many mansions; if it were not so, I would have told you. I go to prepare a place for you. And if I go and prepare a place for you, I will come again and receive you to Myself; that where I am, there you may be also. And where I go you know, and the way you know." Thomas said to Him, "Lord, we do not know where You are going, and how can we know the way" Jesus said to him, "I am the way, the truth, and the life. No one comes to the Father except through Me."

John 16:33: "These things I have spoken to you, that in Me you may have peace. In the world you will have tribulation; but be of good cheer, I have overcome the world."

2 Corinthians 1:3–7: Blessed be the God and Father of our Lord Jesus Christ, the Father of mercies and God of all comfort, who comforts us in all our tribulation, that we may be able to comfort those who are in any trouble, with the comfort with which we ourselves are comforted by God. For as the sufferings of Christ abound in us, so our consolation also abounds through Christ. Now if we are afflicted, it is for your consolation and salvation, which is effective for enduring the same sufferings which we also suffer. Or if we are comforted, it is for your consolation and salvation. And our hope for you is steadfast, because we know that as you are partakers of the sufferings, so also you will partake of the consolation.

2 Corinthians 5:1–9: For we know that if our earthly house, this tent, is destroyed, we have a building from God, a house not made with hands, eternal in the heavens. For in this we groan, earnestly desiring to be clothed with our habitation which is from heaven, if indeed, having been clothed, we shall not be found naked. For we who are in this tent groan, being burdened, not because we want to be unclothed, but further clothed, that mortality may be swallowed up by life. Now He who has prepared us for this very thing is God, who also has given us the Spirit as a guarantee. So we are always confident, knowing that while we are at home in the body we are absent from the Lord. For we walk by faith, not by sight. We are confident, yes, well pleased rather to be absent from the body and to be present with the Lord. Therefore we make it our aim, whether present or absent, to be well pleasing to Him.

Philippians 1:23: For I am hard pressed between the two, having a desire to depart and be with Christ, which is far better.

Philippians 3:20–21: For our citizenship is in heaven, from which we also eagerly wait for the Savior, the Lord Jesus Christ, who will transform our lowly body that it may be conformed to His glorious body, according to the working by which He is able even to subdue all things to Himself.

1 Peter 4:12–13: Beloved, do not think it strange concerning the fiery trial which is to try you, as though some strange thing happened to you; but rejoice to the extent that you partake of Christ's sufferings, that when His glory is revealed, you may also be glad with exceeding joy.

Revelation 7:13–17: Then one of the elders answered, saying to me, "Who are these arrayed in white robes, and where did they come from?" And I said to him, "Sir, you know." So he said to me, "These are the ones who come out of the great tribulation, and washed their robes and made them white in the blood of the Lamb. Therefore they are before the throne of God, and serve Him day and night in His temple. And He who sits on the throne will dwell among them. They shall neither hunger anymore nor thirst anymore; the sun shall not strike them, nor any heat; for the Lamb who is in the midst of the throne will shepherd them and lead them to living fountains of waters. And God will wipe away every tear from their eyes."

Revelation 14:13: Then I heard a voice from heaven saying to me, "Write: 'Blessed are the dead who die in the Lord from now on.'" "Yes," says the Spirit, "that they may rest from their labors, and their works follow them."

The Roman Road to Salvation

1. Romans 3:23: "For all have sinned and fall short of the glory of God." *Because all of us have sinned, we are separated from God.* Not many people will dispute that they have sinned. We all have personal weaknesses and personal guilt. People are naturally self-serving. Even though people do good things, we all have done our share of wrong.

2. Romans 6:23: "For the wages of sin is death, but the gift of God is eternal life in Christ Jesus our Lord." *The consequence of our sin is death.* This verse explains one of the most important concepts of the Bible in one sentence. God is Holy and perfect, without any wrong. He cannot be in the presence of sin. Because we have all sinned, we are all separated from Him. This is much like a limb being cut from a tree; it has been removed from its source of life! We cannot have spiritual life because we have been removed from God because of sin. So if we have all sinned, and God cannot be in the presence of sin, how can we be saved from eternal spiritual death?

3. Romans 5:8: "But God demonstrates His own love toward us, in that while we were still sinners, Christ died for us." *The penalty for our sin was paid by Jesus Christ.* Notice that this verse does not say "God loved us so much that He was really distressed that we were separated from Him by our sin." No! God *demonstrated* His love. He did something in history that proved His love; Jesus Christ died for us. Despite our sinful condition, Christ died for us. This is the wonderful message of the gospel: God loves us despite our sinful condition, so much that He became a man, Jesus Christ, the perfect, holy, and sinless God in the form of man. He came to die in our stead, taking the penalty of our sins (death) on Himself so that we might live the way God intended for us to live: in total dependence on Him and in total obedience to Him.

4. Romans 10:9: "If you confess with your mouth the Lord Jesus and believe in your heart that God has raised Him from the dead, you will be saved." *If we repent of our sinfulness, then confess and trust Jesus Christ as the Lord and Savior of our lives, we will be saved from the penalty of sin.* The gospel offers us a promise, to save us from the penalty of sin; we must believe it. The gospel also offers us a person, Jesus Christ who paid our penalty and who deserves to be Lord of our lives; we must receive Him. I would like to invite you right now to pray to God, telling Him you're ready to trust Christ to save you from the penalty of sin and to confess Him as the Lord over your life. There is a prayer you can pray right now, but let the words be your own; don't just repeat words as if they were a spiritual chant, but speak them to the personal God who loves you enough to die for you. *Lord, I admit that I have sinned and made myself unclean before you, the Holy God. I understand that I deserve death as the penalty for my sins, and I believe that Jesus Christ paid this price with His blood. I want to turn away from my lifestyle of selfishness and sin; I repent. I confess Jesus Christ as my Savior and I put Him in control of my life as my Lord. I pray in Jesus' name, Amen.*

An Alternative Witnessing Plan: The John 3:16 (NASB) One-Verse Method

By Bill Jones

What follows is a step-by-step explanation, including diagrams, for using John 3:16 to share the gospel in personal evangelism.

Introducing the Verse

Transition: John 3:16 is the most famous verse in the entire Bible. May I show you why?

Action: Take out a piece of paper and write the words of John 3:16 at the very top of the page in this particular order. (To help you remember this order, note that the middle two phrases both start with the word "that" and both end with a reference to Jesus Christ.) Number these phrases in the following order: 1, 3, 4, 2.

John 3:16

1. For God so loved the world
3. That He gave His only begotten Son
4. That whoever believes in Him
2. Shall not perish, but have eternal life

Explanation: The reason John 3:16 is so famous is because it summarizes the Bible in four spiritual truths. If you understand these four spiritual truths, you will understand what the entire Bible is all about.

God's Purpose

Transition: Let's look at the first truth.

Action: Put quotation marks around the words "God," "Love," and "World." Then, about half-way down the page, diagram this truth by writing the word "God" on the right, the word "world" on the left, and the word "love" down the middle.

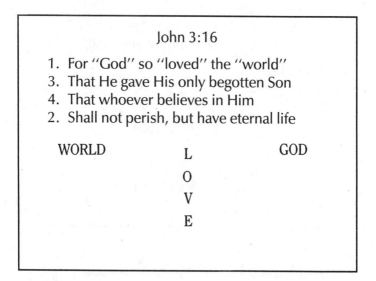

John 3:16

1. For "God" so "loved" the "world"
3. That He gave His only begotten Son
4. That whoever believes in Him
2. Shall not perish, but have eternal life

WORLD   L   GOD
                O
                V
                E

Explanation: God created man to have a personal relationship with Him. He wants this relationship to be one of love—one where God shows His love to people and where people show their love to Him.

Transition: Why do you think that more people are not experiencing this loving personal relationship?

Action: Write the word "sin" below the word "love." Then draw two cliffs, one under the word "world," and the other under the word "God."

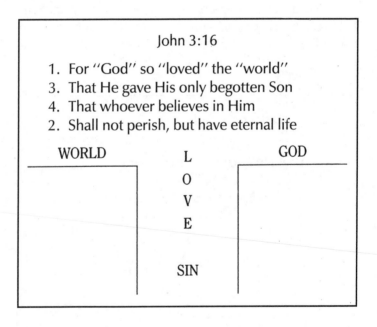

John 3:16

1. For "God" so "loved" the "world"
3. That He gave His only begotten Son
4. That whoever believes in Him
2. Shall not perish, but have eternal life

WORLD   L   GOD
         O
         V
         E

         SIN

Explanation: It is because of sin. Sin is disobeying God. When someone is offended it causes problems in the relationship. Sin causes a separation between God and man.

Man's Problem

Transition: Let's look at the second spiritual truth. It says "shall not perish, but have eternal life."

Action: Put quotation marks around the word "perish" and write it under the left hand cliff, the one with the word "world" on it. Then draw an arrow downward from the word "perish" and write the word "hell."

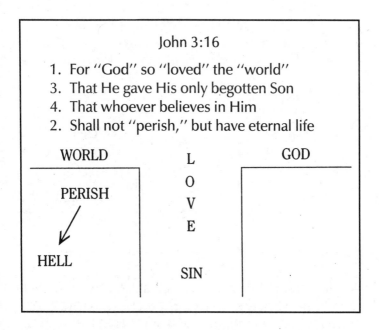

John 3:16

1. For "God" so "loved" the "world"
3. That He gave His only begotten Son
4. That whoever believes in Him
2. Shall not "perish," but have eternal life

WORLD   L   GOD
               O
  PERISH   V
               E
   ↙
HELL   SIN

Explanation: It is bad enough to be separated from God and His love, but it gets worse. The Bible says that if anyone dies physically while spiritually separated from God, he/she will spend eternity in a place called hell.

Transition: That's bad news, but this second spiritual truth also gives some good news.

Action: Put quotation marks around the words "eternal life" and write them under the right hand cliff. Draw an arrow downward and write the word "heaven."

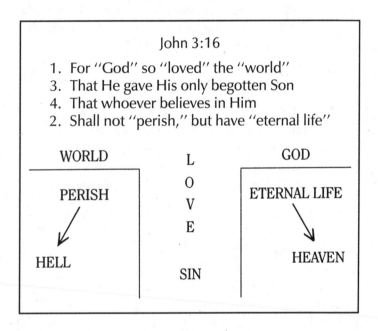

John 3:16

1. For "God" so "loved" the "world"
3. That He gave His only begotten Son
4. That whoever believes in Him
2. Shall not "perish," but have "eternal life"

WORLD	L	GOD
PERISH	O	ETERNAL LIFE
	V	
	E	
HELL		HEAVEN
	SIN	

Explanation: The good news is that God does not want man to spend eternity in hell. His desire is to have a personal relationship with man so that they can live together forever in a place called heaven.

God's Remedy

Transition: The question then becomes: How does one deal with his or her problem of sin? That leads us to the third spiritual truth.

Action: Put quotation marks around the word "Son" and write it on the diagram so that it shares the word "love." Then draw a cross that encloses the words "Son" and "love" and bridge the two cliffs.

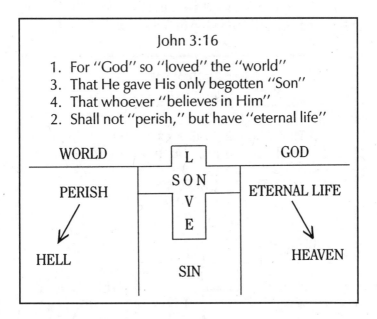

John 3:16

1. For "God" so "loved" the "world"
3. That He gave His only begotten "Son"
4. That whoever "believes in Him"
2. Shall not "perish," but have "eternal life"

WORLD   L   GOD

S O N

PERISH   V   ETERNAL LIFE

E

HELL

SIN

HEAVEN

Explanation: God took care of the sin problem by sending His Son, Jesus Christ, to live a perfect life, then die on the Cross in order that a person's sin could be forgiven. The amazing thing is after Jesus was dead and buried, He rose from the dead, proving God has the power to save people from a destiny of torment.

Man's Response

Transition: The question now is, how can a person cross over the bridge that Christ has provided? The fourth spiritual truth gives the answer.

Action: Draw an arrow from the word "world" to the word "God." Put quotation marks around the words "believes in Him" and write them on top of the arrow.

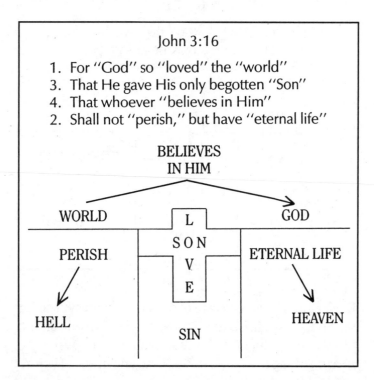

John 3:16

1. For "God" so "loved" the "world"
3. That He gave His only begotten "Son"
4. That whoever "believes in Him"
2. Shall not "perish," but have "eternal life"

BELIEVES
IN HIM

WORLD   L   GOD

                S O N
PERISH   V   ETERNAL LIFE
                E

HELL   SIN   HEAVEN

Explanation: It is not enough to simply know (1) that God loves you, (2) that your sin keeps you from that love and will ultimately send you to hell, and (3) that Jesus Christ's death on the Cross spares you from it all. It is only as you believe in Christ as your Lord and Savior that you cross over the separation caused by your sin and begin a personal relationship with God. This word "believe" is more than just believing in Abraham Lincoln. It means to commit everything you know about yourself to everything you know about Christ. It means to trust Christ and Him alone to make you right with God.

Invitation

Transition: May we personalize this for a moment?

Action: Draw a circle around the word "whoever," then write the word "whoever" above the phrase "believes in Him."

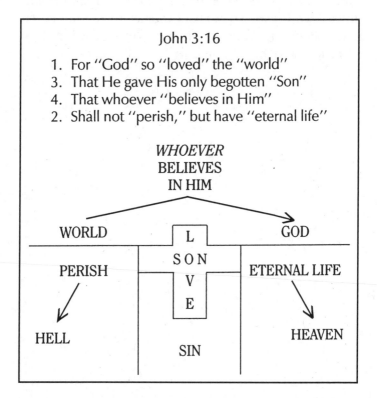

John 3:16

1. For "God" so "loved" the "world"
3. That He gave His only begotten "Son"
4. That whoever "believes in Him"
2. Shall not "perish," but have "eternal life"

WHOEVER
BELIEVES
IN HIM

WORLD   GOD

PERISH   ETERNAL LIFE

L
S O N
V
E

HELL   HEAVEN

SIN

Explanation: The Bible says whoever believes in Him will cross over to God and receive eternal life. Where would you place yourself on this diagram?

!   If they put themselves on the right-hand side, ask
     them to tell you about when and how they crossed
     over.

!   If they put themselves on the left-hand side, or on top
     of the cross, ask the next question.

Do you see anything keeping you from placing your faith
in Christ and crossing over to God right now?

!   If they say "yes," ask them what their questions are
     and deal with them accordingly. If you do not know
     the answer to a question, tell them you will try to find
     out.

!   If they say "no," prepare to lead them in prayer ex-
     pressing their desire to God.

Prayer of Salvation

Transition: If you desire to place your faith in Christ to make you right with God, it's as easy as 1, 2, 3, 4.

Action: Put the number 1 under the right hand cliff, the number 2 under the left hand cliff, the number 3 under the cross, and the number 4 beside the word "whoever."

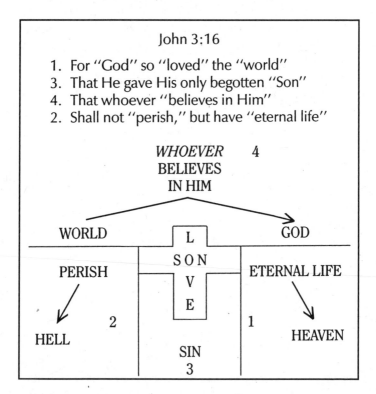

John 3:16

1. For "God" so "loved" the "world"
3. That He gave His only begotten "Son"
4. That whoever "believes in Him"
2. Shall not "perish," but have "eternal life"

WHOEVER 4
BELIEVES
IN HIM

WORLD   GOD

L
S O N
V
E

PERISH   ETERNAL LIFE

2   1

HELL   HEAVEN

SIN
3

Explanation: If you would like to trust Christ you can do so right now. Tell God: (1) that you are grateful that He loves you, (2) that you are sorry for your sin that has separated you from His love, (3) that you are grateful that He gave His only Son to forgive your sin, and (4) that you believe Christ will make you right with Him right now.

I can pray and you can repeat after me. Remember, what is most important is the attitude of your heart, not the words of your mouth. You can pray the right words, but if your heart is not truly convinced that only Christ can make you right with God, then you will not cross over to God. Let's close our eyes and pray right now. (Pray the above four truths back to God.)

Invitations

By Robert J. Morgan

An Invitation to Salvation

During His time on earth, Jesus was always inviting people to become His followers. He said to those by the Sea of Galilee, "Follow me." He invited His listeners to come to Him, to come by faith, to come for healing, to come for hope, to come for happiness. He said, "Come to Me, all you who labor and are heavy laden, and I will give you rest" (Matthew 11:28). He said, "If anyone desires to come after Me, let him deny himself, and take up his cross, and follow Me (Matthew 16:24).

Perhaps today you feel that Christ Himself is speaking just to you. Imagine if He were in this room, giving this invitation. What would you do? He really is in this room. He really is inviting you to become His child, His follower, His disciple. I'm going to ask you to leave your seat and come down one of the aisles. Someone will meet you here and pray with you. Come now. Come willingly. Come courageously. Don't worry about what anyone else thinks; this is your time with Christ. He is calling you as an individual, calling you as a couple, calling you as a family. He died for you and rose again. His blood washes away our sins, and He can give you new life if you'll come. Come to Christ now, while there's still time, while you still can.

Only a step to Jesus!
O why not come and say,
"Gladly to Thee my Savior,
I give myself away."
(Fanny Crosby)

An Invitation to Recommitment

In Revelation 2:4, Jesus warned that the Christians in a particular church had drifted away from their first love; they did not love Him as they once did. Could this apply to you and me today? A little later, in Revelation 3:15, He warned believers in another church that they had grown lukewarm, no longer hot and passionate for Him. Could He mean us? Has your love for Christ waned? Has your devotion to Christ weakened? Has your passion for Him faded? How easily the demands and temptations of the world crowd into our hearts, distracting us from wholehearted obedience to Christ. Today Jesus is standing at the door of your heart, knocking, listening, waiting to be restored as the Lord and Master of your life. I'm going to ask you to renew your commitment to Christ. Repent of your sin, and enthrone Him once again in the center of your heart. He allows no rivals. Proclaim Him Lord alone.

An Invitation to Church Membership

A Christian without a church is like a child without a family or a man without a country. In this cold world of cynicism and criticism, we need a place of love, fellowship, prayer, and happiness. We need the church. Perhaps today you'd like to officially join our church. We'd love to make you a part of our family. Come join us today. If you know Christ as your Savior and you want to make this your "church home," just step out from where you are sitting, come to the front, and someone will be glad to talk and pray with you about it.

If your membership is at another church, it can be transferred here to us. If you've never been baptized, we would be glad to talk with you about the meaning of baptism. If you've been saved and baptized, but have never joined a church, you can become a member here upon the simple statement of your faith in Christ. "Come with us, and we will treat you well; for the Lord has promised good thing" (Numbers 10:29).

◆

An Invitation to Share a Concern with a Pastor

During this time in our worship service, we invite you to share with a pastor (one of our pastors, deacons, altar workers, or staff members) a concern. There is power in praying with another person. Jesus said, Again I say to you that if two of you agree on earth concerning anything that they ask, it will be done for them by My Father in heaven. For where two or three are gathered together in My name, I am there in the midst of them" (Matthew 18:19–20). If there is a specific need in your life, someone here is waiting to pray with you about it. If you'd like to frame it in general terms, that's all right. If you need spiritual guidance in your own life, if you need help, if you need encouragement, or if you need God, please come. Come now. Come and kneel. Come and pray. Come and let us join you at your point of need in Christ's stead and in His name.

An Invitation for Altar Prayer

An old hymn says, "I must tell Jesus all of my trials; I cannot bear these burdens alone." Today we'd like to invite you to join us at the altar, here at the front of the church, for prayer. The Bible tells us to cast all our cares on Him who cares for us. If you have an illness of body, mind, or soul, we invite you to come for prayer. As you come imagine that you are taking that burden, that illness, that hurt, that problem, and laying it here on this altar, on the footstool of the Almighty. Some problems God alone can solve. Some hurts God alone can heal. With those issues, we have to "let go and let God." Bring your burden to the Lord and leave it here. If you'd like to come and pray privately, you may. If you'd like someone to pray with you, there's someone waiting to do so. Just step out, come, kneel, give Christ your burden, and receive His strength. Cast your care upon the Lord and He will sustain you. He shall never permit the righteous to be moved (Psalm 55:22).

✦

An Invitation to Dedication to Christian Service

We know that God gives every Christian a personal ministry; He has a purpose for us all. Ephesians 4:7 tells us that God has given each one of us a spiritual gift for use in His kingdom's work. But God calls some to a special task, some as evangelists, some as pastors, some as missionaries, some in other roles. And when He calls us, we must go. Where He leads us, we must follow. What He tells us, we must do. There is no greater calling than to be fully dedicated to the Lord for His service during our fleeting days on this earth. If you sense that God's calling you to Christian service, won't you yield? Won't you come? Today I invite you to come in full surrender, to come forward to this altar and say, "Lord, here am I. Send me."